SECURING THE FUTURE
OF THE USA AND THE PLANET

Ronex James John Kennedy Mute*Shael's*
Global Revolution
Awakening the USA to its authentic global leadership role!

A manifesto in support of the 99% of the USA and the planet:
- The Occupy Wall Street Revolutionaries
- The Tea Partiers
- The fed up Democrats
- The fed up Republicans
- The fed up Christian and non-Christian
- The fed up whoever you are

Ronex Kennedy Mutesha, Ph.D. (Engg-abd)
B.Min.Sc.(Engg), M.S.(Engg), M.S.(O.M.-abt), Ph.D.(Engg-abd)

"Success is deep-rooted in what you can do for others to enhance their lives"

SECURING THE FUTURE OF THE USA AND THE PLANET
A manifesto in support of the 99% of the USA and the planet!

Excerpts from the following books:

"*Ron*ex James *John Kennedy* Mute*Shael's* Glo**bal** R**e**volution
Awakening the USA to its authentic global leadership role!"
and
"Unlocking Higher Performance—Learning from 24/7 Smart Billionaires & Millionaires"

Copyright © 2011 by Ronex Kennedy Mutesha Ph.D. (Engg-abd)

Published by the Ronex James John Kennedy Muteshael Publications

Picture taken by: Charlotte Chimbini Nyirenda-Mutesha
Cover Design: Ronex Kennedy Mutesha

All rights reserved. No part of this book may be reproduced without written permission, except for brief quotations in books and critical reviews.

First Printing, 2011, Printed in the USA

Unless otherwise noted, Scripture quotations are taken from the Holy Bible:
New King James Version (NKJV) © 1984 by Thomas Nelson, Inc.

*****Library of Congress Cataloging-in-Publication Data*****

Mutesha, Ronex Kennedy, 1959-
SECURING THE FUTURE OF THE USA AND THE PLANET
A Manifesto/Ronex Kennedy Mutesha— 1st. ed.
p. cm.

ISBN 978-1-257-65790-2
1. History/Public Policies/Government/Business/Economics/Social/Spiritual/Leadership

Ronex James John Kennedy Muteshael Publications books are available at special discounts for the purpose of helping people who cannot afford the going price and bulk purchases for employees and students. For other books, resources and products offered and more info:

e-mail us at: ronexkm@gmail.com
or write to:
**Ronex James John Kennedy Muteshael,
24/7 SmartG.R.O.U.P.Network™**
421 S. Humphrey Avenue,
Oak Park, IL 60302. USA
or go to:
http://www.RonexOnline.Com.

Join us on Facebook.: **Ronex Kennedy Mutesha: 24/7 SmartG.R.O.U.P.Network™**

Our Skype I.D. is: **ronexkennedy.mutesha**

DEDICATION

To my children Andy Zimba Mutesha, Charlotte Chimbini Mutesha, Chloé Balekile Mutesha, and Dumisani Thompson James Mutesha (Zeke), all the children of the world to whom we owe a safer and better world of tomorrow, and the 99% of the USA and the Planet.

SECURING THE FUTURE OF THE USA AND THE PLANET

A manifesto in support of the 99% of the USA and the planet!

Table of Contents

TOPIC — **PAGE**

INTRODUCTION — 7
- An Inevitable National And Global Revolution: The Rise of the 99%—Class Warfare. — 7
- A call to unity among all Americans and citizens of the planet of all walks of life. — 13
- 235 years later the USA is still dysfunctional! — 17
- Can we secure the USA outside of a global context? — 17
- Gross Human Rights Violations through the U.S. Constitution. — 18
- A dysfunctional government system disapproved by 85% of ordinary Americans. — 18
- Ostracizing God from the public arena—how has that worked for the USA? — 18
- Based on the U.S. Constitution we are not a Christian Nation! — 19
- Who can change Washington D.C.? No human being can! — 20
- Have we chosen our leaders wisely? How do we do that? — 20
- Repealing the U.S. Constitution in its entirety! First thing first. — 21
- Forgiving our founding fathers and moving forward. — 21
- Today, what would Y'shua the Messiah say to most of us? — 21

CHAPTER
1. AM I REINCARNATED BASED ON MY NAMES: **RON**EX JAMES *JOHN KENNEDY* MUTE*SHAEL*? — 25
2. My 24/7 Smart Performance Improvement Tools. — 35
3. My Objective/Mission. — 39
4. Prophetic Destiny of the U.S. Uttered by Benjamin Franklin. — 43
5. Proof Positive that the U.S. Constitution has failed to work for ordinary Americans—The 14 Factors. — 45
6. RJJKM'S GLOBAL REVOLUTION—Awakening the USA to its authentic global leadership role. — 47
7. My Mentors Within The Context of My Names: **Ron**ex James *John Kennedy* Mute*Shael* —The Mission Within. — 49
8. Dysfunctions/Woes/Problems Facing The USA And The Planet. — 59
9. Re-founding the USA. — 63
10. Consequences of Deviating From Real Free Enterprise. — 73
11. Presidential Candidates for 2012 including Mr. Barack Obama are ill-equipped to fix what's wrong in the US and around the planet. — 81
12. Act Now To Avert Inevitable Worst World Wide Economic Disasters And Uprisings. — 83

INTRODUCTION

An Inevitable National And Global Revolution:
The Rise of the 99%—Class Warfare

Welcome to securing the future of the United States and the planet manifesto. I am not here in this manifesto to entertain, but because we have serious and urgent issues here in the United States and as a global community to address. So serious that it is a matter of life and death.

My primary goal for this manifesto is not to seek your vote for president of the United States, but to point out root causes of dysfunctions, we see in all essential systems of life, which may lead to a total collapse of these systems in spite of all advancements we have gained thus far.

It is imperative for you after you read this material that you share the information with everyone you know in the United States and all over the world. I want us to take action as a team to remove these dysfunctions peacefully in love and unity for all Americans and other citizens of the planet NOW.

Friends I have been a victim of corporate greed with all the education to Ph.D. level, industry and business experience I have. I have gone without a job and at the same time trying to support a family of five. I have worked at low paying jobs and yes, minimum wage jobs. I have been in the middle class making about $50,000 per year and paying higher taxes than the top 1%, barely making it while I designed quality and productivity improvement systems that helped companies acquire more business, reduce cost, improve profits, etc., while I was underpaid into servitude. I know the first thing about trying to survive.

Having been a small business owner, I know first hand how hard it is to start a business and survive when access to the capital you need to operate your business is limited to the privileged top 1%.

I have worked for companies doing as low as $10 million and as much as billions of dollars per year, and though I understand how hard it is to compete, most of them are driven by greed. The victim is always the employee.

Very few politicians and lawyers can relate to the 99% as much as I can and that is the reason why I created all the resources I did to help the 99% of us rise out these ashes we have been dumped into by the top 1%.

My name is Ronex James John Kennedy MuteShael. Yes, two of my middle names are John Kennedy.

In 1961, John Fitzgerald Kennedy was <u>44</u> years old when he became president of the United States.

I was born on April 7th, 1959, a Good Friday—1 year and 7 months before JFK was elected president in November of 1960.

In 2003 when I was <u>44</u> years old by the grace of Almighty God I predicted that president #<u>44</u> of these United States was going to be a Black man.

It was in 2003 at the age of 44 when I received my global mission:

www.RonexOnline.Com.:
The Ronex James John Kennedy Muteshael
24/7 SmartGROUPNetwork™

Without thinking about it, I registered my domain name RonexOnline.Com on April 7, 2011 exactly 1 year and 7 months before the November 2012 presidential election.

When between April 7th, 2003, my birthday and May 29th, 2003 JFK's birthday, I predicted that **President #44 of these United States will be a Black man,** people didn't believe me—including my own family. This prediction was before I knew anything about Mr. Barack Obama and it was before his speech at the DNC of 2004. A prediction against a backdrop that John Kerry was running to become president #44.

To make the above prediction even more divine, between December 4th and 5th of 2003 I predicted that **Mr. George W. Bush, president #43 would get a second term in office**. Political pundits said George W. would be a one term president like his father.

Imagine the chances of above predictions coming true against all odds **within 5 years**. Both the re-election and election of George W. and Barack respectively **were historical**.

In 2001 right after September 11, 2001, based on my discovery of the fact that the top 1% of the population owned 40% of wealth in the United States, I decided to write my book, entitled "Unlocking Higher Performance—Learning from 24/7 Smart Billionaires and Millionaires™" for three reasons,

- firstly, *to help us improve performance as individuals or as an organization*,
- secondly *to help change the wealth distribution landscape from the top 1% of the population owning 40% to a <u>bigger percent</u> of the population owning wealth in America* and
- thirdly, *to help create more jobs in America and to reach out to the poor of the planet*.

For me this was really the beginning of my global revolution I decided to call the Ronex James John Kennedy Muteshael's Global Revolution. This is my giving back to America and God's planet, but cannot be a one-man show.

In 2003 I started my own version of **Occupy Wall Street**. I peacefully demonstrated against corporate greed at least three times at International Profit Associates (IPA) in Buffalo Grove, Illinois, United States where I was underpaid into servitude. The last time I demonstrated on September 9, 2008 I was arrested, charges were fabricated and I was imprisoned for more than 2 years. My **Occupy IPA** was a foreshadowing of **Occupy Wall Street**.

Friends all essential aspects of life are dysfunctional right here in the United States and around the world. By the grace of God, I saw all this coming, way back in 2001. The situation is so scary and imperative that when I launched my website April 7, 2011, on it, I said and I quote,

> "To get these United States functioning again it will take, not only a national revolution, but a global one as the woes we face today are global. Until the truth is told as to why we have dysfunctions, our slide in the conduit that leads to the abyss of self-destruction continues."

Three months later in July of 2011, a Canadian consumer advocate launched **Occupy Wall Street**. The movement has spread across the United States. There is a global revolution going on right now all over the world.

Today 99% of Americans are victims of corporate greed—slaves, if you will, to the top 1% that are rich and powerful in the United States that own 40% of its wealth. How did this happen? We can find the answer to this question in the history of the United States and the planet.

Are my predictions and their fulfillment a coincidence as to what has happened thus far? Absolutely not! Are my life experiences and background a coincidence as to being appropriate to our circumstances at such a time as this? Absolutely not!

The issue of slavery in the United States was ignored by the first 16 presidents of the United States, including Abraham Lincoln until after 625,000 people died during the Civil War. How can this happen in a nation which claims to be a Christian nation?

Class warfare is inevitable—the top 1% versus the 99%. What will be the cost of this warfare? If in fact violence erupted between the 99%, which is 308,000,000 Americans against the top 1% or 3,000,000 other Americans who are rich because the 99% come to believe that the top 1% doesn't really care about the approximately 308,000,000 (the 99%), what would be the cost in human life? What would be the implication economically and financially? The United States would come to a complete stop since the top 1% rides on the backs of the 99% to obscenely profit from enslaving them.

Again, how can we allow this deterioration to anarchy in all essential aspects of life in a nation which claims to be a Christian nation?

Every election year there is talk about who is a Christian and who is not, among those running for the office of the President of the United States. And yet based on the Constitution of the United States we have separation of Church and State—meaning the government of the United States is secular in its endeavors. The question now becomes: Can a true Christian carry out the affairs of the United States successfully? The answer is no. Can we pray for a secular government and seriously expect the God who was revealed by the Christ to answer our prayers? No.

I strongly believe that a lot of us who follow the Christ intimately and otherwise have sincerely prayed to God asking for His blessing on the United States—God bless the USA. 235 years later as a nation, the USA is more dysfunctional than it ever was. My logical and analytical mind tells me God is not answering our prayers. If not, why not?

- Therefore one of my goals in this manifesto is to show that we can't secure the future of the USA because it is secular in its operation.
- My second goal is to prove that the word of God is true and that the USA has been used by God to prove that fact.
- The third goal is to categorically prove that, if in fact God is true to His word, the only way we can secure the USA and any nation on the planet is with the aid of Almighty God. How do we do that?

It is for all the above that I have chosen to provide my analysis of our predicament from especially the point of view of what the Holy Scriptures say foremost and then use my education, industry and business experience to layout a framework within which we should operate to guarantee peace and prosperity for our future generations.

Why should you listen to me? Foremost is the fact that I am not in the top 1% and that I can relate to the 99% because I have been there and did my own version of Occupy Wall Street. I care about the 99% based on my own experience with corporate greed. I also realize that we live in a culture where everybody claims they are better qualified than somebody else based various criteria and so when I say that I am more:

- extensively educated to Ph.D. level than all presidents we have had including Mr. Barack Obama, and that
- I have more extensive industry and business experience than all presidents we have had including Mr. Barack Obama, and that
- I have had better top performance in both school and industry where I have been than all presidents we have had including Mr. Barack Obama, I am not boasting or being an ego-maniac or narcissistic, but stating a fact.

Nobody among those who have declared their candidacy for the office of the president of the USA can match my background. Nobody among those in the Congress of the USA can match my background. At this time nobody in the USA can match my background. In fact, at this time, nobody on the planet can match my background.

The USA and the rest of the planet combined is a complex system of individual, national and global endeavors. Figuring out how it has worked in the past and how it works today and determining what is dysfunctional to brainstorm solutions, the president, of especially the USA, needs to be adequately familiar with how all essential aspects of life interact through real life industry experience and education.

We have reached a level of dysfunction so much that there is no one I can think of in the United States and on the planet that can understand the complexity of our dilemma we face better than I can.

My extensive educational background to Ph.D level, extensive industrial and business management experience in essential industries sets me apart from every president that has ever been elected to the presidency of the USA—in fact on the whole planet.

I obtained my Bachelor's degree in Mining Engineering at the UNIVERSITY OF ZAMBIA in Lusaka, Zambia, Africa. The UNIVERSITY OF ZAMBIA is an *arts, natural sciences and engineering university.*

Graduating with Distinction, highest honors, a GPA equivalent to a 4.0 out of a 4.0 scale in 1983, I was in the top 2% of the graduating class.

During my undergrad, I took courses from the Chemistry, Physics, Mechanical Engineering, Civil Engineering, Electrical Engineering, Metallurgical Engineering, Geological Engineering, Mining Engineering and Computer Science Departments, etc.

I obtained my Master of Science degree in Mining Engineering with concentration in Operations & Small Business Management in 1986 at MICHIGAN TECHNOLOGICAL UNIVERSITY in HOUGHTON, MICHIGAN, United States.

After completing course requirements for both my second Master of Science and Ph.D. degrees in the School of Business and Engineering administration and Mining Engineering, that is, Master of Science in Operations Management—all but thesis and Ph.D. Engineering—all but dissertation with a cumulative graduate GPA of 3.75 out of a 4.0 scale, highest honors, in 1988, I decided to have industry and business management experience.

Over the entire course of my life I have been a part of Christian churches and other non-profits, volunteering, the latest of which are as a Small Group Leader at Willow Creek Community Church in South Barrington, Illinois, USA—One of the fastest growing churches in north America.

I volunteered on the Procurement Strategic Planning Task Force of World Vision located in Chicago, Illinois, United States and other faith-based and non-profit organizations not as famous. You can find my summary of accomplishments on my website at: www.ronexonline.com and in my book, "Unlocking Higher Performance—Learning from 24/7 Smart Billionaires and Millionaires™".

USA Civil and Criminal law experience

Over the years I have litigated cases as a pro se attorney in civil court and had one case settled out of court.

During the two years and three months that I was incarcerated, I studied criminal law using the computer law library Lexus Nexus at Lake County Jail in Waukegan, Illinois. I did more than 60 one-on-one legal and spiritual counseling sessions for fellow inmates. I did more than 30 legal defense motions in about four months. Through motions I did for inmates, for some I was able to get charges against them dropped and for some their sentences were reduced.

Self-Taught—The Constitution of the United States

While at Lake County Jail I studied the Constitution of the United States. I have never worked for a company that never needed any productivity and quality improvement—all of them did, whether doing a few million dollars a year or a billion dollars. The Constitution of the United States was constructed by our founding fathers who were riding horses to attend the inauguration ceremony at the White House—technology has advanced tremendously. Our nation is diverse.

One thing remains constant—the Constitution of United States rejected God by opting for secularism—the biggest mistake, hence the woes we face today within and without.

Again I want to say this that, there is no politician present or past that can match or beat my background. I am not saying this for self-glorification or to down others, but to say that I am the most qualified for the presidency of the United States. But, would I choose to run with the Constitution of the United States as is? No I wouldn't because in spite of my impeccable background I couldn't change Washington D.C. in my power, for I know that only the Almighty alone is able to bring about change in human beings—not I, realizing that He does it through us.

When the Almighty brings **_change_** to Washington D.C, through all of us acknowledging our ultimate dependency on Him, only then can the United States avert self-induced destructive events within and without brought about through our secular ideologies.

In short I am a proactive, results and action oriented professional in business building and management. More than that is the fact that I have been a student of the Bible all my life. In the last 2 years I have read the Bible twice. I am going through it the third time. The Bible has proven itself as the word of the Almighty through my life experiences and history of the United States. My study of science, engineering and business, and my industry experience has authenticated the existence of an orderly Almighty God who was revealed by Y'shua the Messiah.

What the above background means is that, it is not a coincidence that I am already doing what the president of the USA is supposed to be doing. And if we had such a thing as the president of the world, I am already doing what such a person should be doing—I am reaching out to other peoples of the planet for, it is in all of us citizens of the planet working together as a team that we will be able to address various issues facing us at the national and global level.

A call to unity and love among all Americans and citizens of the planet of all walks of life

I want to preface this section by saying that my applied science, that is, engineering and business background in addition to my personal unexplainable supernatural experiences have led me to the conclusion with certainty, beyond a shadow of doubt, that the God who proclaimed spiritual laws in the Holy Scriptures of the Bible is the author of science, all engineering laws and free enterprise.

It is a well known fact that anybody who tries to buck the law of gravity by jumping off a tall building may end up dead or hurt physically, but we have this belief about spiritual laws that we can violate them and not suffer consequences. In our evaluation of our economical and financial systems and other systems we refuse to accept the fact that there is a possibility and probability that our financial bankruptcy and economic dysfunction may be directly related to violating spiritual laws.

More than ever we must unite because divisiveness and hatred are the ingredients that are destroying the US and Planet Earth. The United States of America and the whole world has reached the epitome in dysfunction and by all accounts from the point of view of economical, political, foreign policy, judicial, social, moral and spiritual systems in place, as citizens of the planet we are on the edge of the cliff about to jump into our demise.

I am calling on ordinary American citizens—Republicans, Democrats, Tea Partiers, Independents, Centrists, Occupy Wall Street revolutionaries to join me in this national and global revolution that has engulfed the whole planet to unity in love so we can allow the Almighty to bring about change that only God is capable of actualizing when we operate under the unconditional love for all humanity including the rich and powerful at this juncture of our lives as human beings on the planet. We cannot allow bloodshed if at all possible.

Realizing that there is no language that speaks louder than unconditional love for humanity—both sinner and saint, it is the only language that can unite all of us. We all understand love for our immediate families for which we are passionate about, that we do all we can to provide for and protect them. There is no human being on the planet that will not respond to a genuine extension of love. That is why the greatest spiritual leader of all time said love of our neighbor as ourselves and loving Almighty God are the greatest commandments in the Holy Bible.

If in fact the basis of all religions and spiritual belief systems should be love, we all understand to an extent who God is—God is love hence the reason why we all respond to love overwhelmingly positive. We are divisive, deceptive, depraved, exploitative, destructive and evil in our deportment toward one another because we don't comprehend what love really is.

Because I know for sure that Y'shua the Messiah would reach out to every human being on the planet and extend His unconditional love to all of us if He was walking in the flesh on the planet today, I am reaching out and extending my unconditional love to all humanity in the USA and all nations on the planet—both saint and so-called sinner, which we all are. Y'shua is the Hebrew name for Jesus Christ. I will be using Y'shua in this address because I love the Hebrew name.

In John 17:20-26 (NKJV), Y'shua prays for unity and love among believers right here on earth, not when He comes back, as a sign to the world to show that He was sent by God our Father in Heaven. The passage says and I quote:

> "I do not pray for these alone, but also for those who will believe in Me through their word; that ***they all may be one***, as You, Father, *are* in Me, and I in You; that ***they also may be one in Us***, that ***the world may believe that You sent Me***. And the ***glory which You gave Me I have given them, that they may be one just as We are one***: I in them, and You in Me; that they ***may be made perfect in one***, and that ***the world may know that You have sent Me***, and have ***loved them as You have loved Me***. "Father, I desire that they also whom You gave Me may be with Me where I am, that they may behold My glory which You have given Me; for You loved Me before the foundation of the world. O righteous Father! The world has not known You, but I have known You; and these have known that You sent Me. ***And I have declared to them Your name, and will declare it, that the love with which You loved Me may be in them, and I in them.***"

Contribution to progress, though it came through some human beings being sacrificed to satiate the few who are demonically greedy, has come from all races, ethnicities, religions, languages, colors, sexes, sexual orientations, etc.—all humanity must be appreciated.

However, I need to add that, in the exact same way that we cannot break the laws of science without suffering consequences, breaking spiritual laws leads to various dysfunctions including economic, financial, health-related ones, etc.

Holy Scriptures speak against greed and worship of the Almighty Dollar and we all know that our stock markets are driven by fear of losing money and greed. How has that worked for us?

Politics are driven by deception and divisiveness contrary to the teaching of scripture, it is no wonder government is dysfunctional.

Our adversarial justice system is not justice for all—it is justice for all the rich and powerful and injustice for all the poor and middle classes of all races, especially Black people contrary to the teaching of scripture—a justice system that condones fib-telling is dysfunctional in addition to violating scripture.

If in fact our dysfunctional justice system is the conduit through which we legislate all laws that govern how we conduct ourselves in all essential aspects of life, the result is a dysfunctional society here in the USA and around the world.

I know that most of you know the answer to the following question: What is the solution to all the woes we face? Or should I ask: What is the root cause of all the woes we face? I will be very precise in giving you the answer to the second question. One word—SECULARISM. The answer to the first question is also summarized in one word—GOD. What a new concept? No it is not a new concept—read 1 Samuel 8:4-21(NKJV) in the Bible. Are kings, queens, presidents, prime ministers and religious leaders who are not guided by scripture today really in it for the subjects, peasants, the middle class or the poor? No. They are in it for themselves. The biggest experiments in man-made exploitative capitalism, communism, fascism, etc., and so-called western democracies have failed—fulfilling God's prophecy about how kings, queens, presidents, prime ministers and religious leaders who are not guided by scripture would behave toward those who put them in office.

1 Samuel 8:4-21(NKJV) says and I quote,

> "Then all the elders of Israel gathered together and came to Samuel at Ramah, and said to him, "Look, you are old, and your sons do not walk in your ways. ***Now make us a king to judge us like all the nations.***" But the thing displeased Samuel when they said, "Give us a king to judge us." So Samuel prayed to the Lord. And the Lord said to Samuel, "Heed the voice of the people in all

that they say to you; for they have not rejected you, **_but they have rejected Me_**, that I **_should not reign over them_**. According to all the works which they have done since the day that I brought them up out of Egypt, even to this day—**_with which they have forsaken Me and served other gods_**—so they are doing to you also. Now therefore, heed their voice. However, you shall solemnly **_forewarn_** them, and show them **_the behavior of the king who will reign over them_**." So Samuel told all the words of the Lord to the people who asked him for a king. And he said, "This will be the behavior of the king who will reign over you: **_He will take your sons and appoint them for his own chariots_** and *to be* his horsemen, and *some* will run before his chariots. He will appoint captains over his thousands and captains over his fifties, **_will set some to plow his ground and reap his harvest_**, and *some* to make his weapons of war and equipment for his chariots. He will take your daughters *to be* perfumers, cooks, and bakers. And he will take the best of your fields, your vineyards, and your olive groves, and give *them* to his servants. He will take a tenth of your grain and your vintage, and give it to his officers and servants. **_And he will take your male servants, your female servants, your finest young men, and your donkeys, and put them to his work._** He will take a tenth of your sheep. And you will be his servants. **_And you will cry out in that day because of your king whom you have chosen for yourselves, and the Lord will not hear you in that day._**" Nevertheless the people refused to obey the voice of Samuel; and they said, "No, but we will have a king over us, that we also may be like all the nations, and that our king may judge us and go out before us and fight our battles." And Samuel heard all the words of the people, and he repeated them in the hearing of the Lord. So the Lord said to Samuel, "Heed their voice, and make them a king.""

There and then the children of Israel were allowed to be ruled by a king and in essence enslaved by the king they desired—king Saul.

The founding fathers of our nation, these United States, rejected the tyrannical rule of the king of Great Britain. Upon independence through the Constitution of the United States, not only was slavery legalized and the freedom of slaves criminalized, Caucasian women were counted as 3/5th of a person and personal property to those they were married as slaves were. Other Caucasians considered inferior became indentured slaves—voting rights were denied to both Caucasian women and slaves. The same imperialistic and exploitative capitalistic system of government that was condemned by the founding fathers was instituted right here in the United States.

When the top 1% (about 3,000,000) of the population owns 40% of wealth and dictate the affairs of about 308,000,000 Americans it is no less than slavery in modern day USA—CAPITALISM.

Free enterprise is not exploitative capitalism, it's God's way of doing business. Isaiah 48:17-18 (NKJV) the prophet quotes God saying, and I quote,

"I am the LORD your God who teaches you to profit."

God is not against legitimate business profit—He is against greed and exploitation of others—stealing other people's labor or underpaying employees into servitude. That is why all *isms* must fail.

What don't we understand about all the above based on the teachings of the Holy Bible and factual evidence available to us today?

235 years later the USA is still dysfunctional!

I want all of us ordinary citizens of the United States and the planet to understand issues from the economical, political, foreign policy, judicial, social, moral and spiritual point of view to identify the root causes of problems we face today.

Our politicians have told us they can fix dysfunctions in Washington D. C. for 235 years—they are still at it. Unfortunately church and other spiritual leaders, evangelical and otherwise have failed to provide spiritual and moral guidance and vision for our country the USA and the planet as they are also caught up in the worship of the Almighty Dollar getting wealthy without taxation. If in fact that is the situation, which it is, the situation is so serious that we must act NOW.

Can we secure the USA outside of a global context?

I am going to give you a summary of how we can **SECURE THE FUTURE OF THE USA** in this discussion—details will be in my book **"*Ronex James John Kennedy* Mute*Shael's* Glo*bal* R*evolution*—Awakening the USA to its authentic global leadership role."**

The other question is: Can the United States secure its future on its own within and outside its borders? The quick answer to that is: ABSOLUTELY NOT! Why do I say that? To answer that question you have to go back to the beginning of our beloved United States before 1776, through 1776 and 1787. In fact to understand why we are fighting a losing battle securing the future of the United States, we have to go back to the beginning—GENESIS in the Sacred writings of the Holy Hebrew Scriptures of God Almighty.

Gross Human Rights Violations through the U.S. Constitution

The history of the United States is replete with factual evidence showing the impossibility of securing the future of the United States outside of a global context and ***without the aid of God***. The essence of the activities of our nation has remained principally the same because of the Constitution of the United States that was drafted in gross violation of human rights—those of Caucasian women who were not allowed to vote and were considered property, African slaves who were not only exploited of their labor but tortured and killed in some situations when they protested against the indignities of their plight, Native Americans and other ethnicities and languages that were considered inferior by the drafters of the Constitution of the United States—our founding fathers.

The U.S. Constitution as is, is a reminder of above gross violations of human rights and total disrespect of God Almighty, hence it will never work. If God was to allow it to work, He would be endorsing a system that continues to violate His enduring principles defined in the pages of scripture. God is showing us in no uncertain terms that violating His spiritual laws, not only results in spiritual bankruptcy, but economic and financial bankruptcy among other things, as a nation.

A dysfunctional government system disapproved by 85% of ordinary Americans.

More important and above the violation of human rights as defined by human beings is the blatant disrespect for the enduring principles of Almighty God. The pure unadulterated justice as defined by the word of God was substituted with, in reality, justice for all the rich and powerful and injustice for all the poor and middle classes of all races, especially Black people.

An inauthentic pretend legislative system was instituted to serve the rich and powerful instead of ordinary Americans of all races and party affiliation.

A government system as set up by our founding fathers consisting of the Judicial arm, Congress and the Executive branch which was deliberately designed to be dysfunctional has reached the epitome of dysfunction as evidenced by the recent debate on the budget and the consequential disapproval rating of 85% of Congress by ordinary Americans. Down grading the US credit rating from its AAA status is another of many evidentially factors. This dysfunction has played out since, the first president, George Washington took office in 1789.

Ostracizing God from the public arena—how has that worked for the USA?

The fact is, as is, even without invoking the enduring principles of God, the Constitution of the United States is what has brought us here and was responsible for 625,000 people dying during the Civil War—Black, White, native Americans and others. Left as is, it is delusional to think that government will ever be functional to serve ordinary Americans—the poor, middle class and legitimate business owners of all sizes.

When we bring into the picture the fact that, even though we operate a secular government in our effort to ostracize God from getting involved in our affairs as human beings, it is absolutely impossible to get rid of God. God is in charge as we have proven to ourselves that, after all, we are not all that smart and are not in control of our lives. If we were able to control our lives with all the economists, engineers, CEOs, scientists, preachers, prophets, psychologists, psychiatrists, psychics, doctors, technologies, innovativeness, ingenuity, etc., we have on the planet right now, we wouldn't be where we are today. The only control we have is that which God allows us to have.

What is worse, in our society today and going back to the beginning of our nation the United States, is that our spiritual leaders, evangelical and otherwise, are toothless bull dogs preaching watered down versions of the gospel of Y'shua having no real impact on government as government has incapacitated them by allowing them to become wealthy without taxation.

Based on the U.S. Constitution we are not a Christian Nation!

Based on the Constitution of the United States, we are not a Christian nation as some of us have been misled to believe. The Constitution of the United States is **supreme to the Bible** as we all know. You cannot be a Christian and believe in the Constitution of the United States for all the above reasons and more. With that in mind and as fact, can we sincerely ask God's divine intervention? The Constitution of the U.S. runs the United States government. Through the U.S. Constitution our founding fathers rejected God, how can we ask God to bless the U.S. government when there is separation of church and state?

We are where we are today because our founding fathers rejected God. I applaud Mr. Rick Perry for trying to ask God's divine intervention just before launching out his campaign for the presidency. We must think God is a fool and as hypocritical as we are to answer our prayers when the U.S. Constitution is our bible.

Can Mr. Perry fix what he believes is partially broken from his human biased perspective instead of God's perspective? Simply stated: Rick can't fix the dysfunction in Washington D.C. because he doesn't know how broken it really is—spiritually among other things. In addition, his animal science degree is inadequate for him to understand the complex nature of the United States and the planet.

I want to make sure everyone is very clear as to why my involvement in this scenario today that has become precarious to ordinary Americans and other citizens of Planet Earth, that I would care less about running for the presidency if the entire Constitution of the United States is not repealed and a new one established. A new one that eliminates dysfunctions that were embedded in the old one by design and/or oversight by the founding fathers.

Who can change Washington D.C.? No human being can!

Forty three presidents of the United States, including Mr. Barack Obama have failed to change Washington D.C. Rick Perry, Mitt Romney, Michele Bachmann, Herman Cain, Newt Gingrich, and everyone else running must think they are gods to insinuate they can change the ways of Washington D.C.—that is, its chosen way of conducting the affairs of American people and other citizens of the planet through secularism. Simply put CONFUSION of the highest order. This confusion—which has reared its ugly head through **d**ivisiveness, **d**eception and **d**epravity—the three "d"s of Washington D.C. representing **d**emons of Washington D.C., was, has and will always be there if we don't repeal a Constitution that rejects God through the first amendment. This dysfunction causing confusion perpetuated by the U.S. Constitution has been epitomized by the fact that an African American is president of the United States today.

I would be delusional to contemplate that as a Black man born in Zambia, Africa, even with my impeccable background, would be able to change Washington, D.C. which operates in the arena of the devil himself, where the three demons abound—divisiveness, deception and depravity.

Have we chosen our leaders wisely? How do we do that?

When leadership rejects divine guidance based on the enduring principles of Yahweh in His sacred writings of Hebrew Scriptures of the Holy Bible, it is God Himself who causes confusion among us—God has confounded us because we have obstinately rejected Him and done what is not right in His sight—our leadership till today have not been blameless in their actions, as God demands of all of us. Unfortunately the sins of our leaders are visiting us—4th generation USA and 28th generation on the planet from the time of Y'shua—it is all in the Holy Bible.

Therefore until the United States chooses its leaders wisely based on what the Bible teaches and operates under the enduring principles of Almighty God, we shall remain confounded. In my book mentioned above and the upcoming one, I briefly explain how the LORD Yahweh anoints His leaders so they can do what is right in His sight, which means—**taking care of the elderly and the poor of all races and yes establishing a free enterprise system, where everybody is allowed to participate and resources are made available to all without regard to race or any other factor that is not based on equity**.

Repealing the U.S. Constitution in its entirety! First thing first

A new U.S. Constitution means a better Covenant with all Americans of all walks of life and a better world. We can't wait until 2012 to repeal the entire Constitution of the United States, humble ourselves before Almighty God, repent of our leaders' sins and begin the re-founding of the United States based on a New Constitution of the United States designed to operate within the guidelines of the enduring principles of the Holy Bible.

When we choose to operate within the guidelines of the enduring principles of the Holy Bible, all our systems would be based on being **radically inclusive**, of all Americans of all races, languages, colors, religious persuasions, nationalities, income levels, sexes and yes sexual orientations, as Y'shua was and would be today giving everyone an opportunity to grow from **grace to grace** as we all extend **unconditional love and tolerance** unto each other knowing that we all do not attain spiritual maturity at the same time.

Forgiving our founding fathers and moving forward.

As grossly miscalculating as our founding fathers were in the framing of the Constitution of the United States, we all must extend our forgiveness to them NOW and once and for all. However, to move forward from this point forth we must repent of all iniquities perpetrated then and turn from and repent of those being perpetuated today. The message from the Almighty couldn't be any clearer or louder than we have seen or heard from pandemic pestilences or plagues, economic dysfunctions and wars among other things we see today within the United States and around the world.

The Constitution of the U.S. has been a symbol and a reminder of exploitation and oppression to many people of all backgrounds and today it still is to the 99%. To embrace a New America we must bid farewell to the old.

Today, what would Y'shua the Messiah say to most of us:
- Spiritual leaders?
- Politicians and lawyers?
- Business men and women?
- Wall Street tycoons?
- Judges?

Spiritual leaders
If Y'shua the Messiah was to say something about most of our spiritual leaders today HE WOULD SAY: DECEPTIVE, DIVISIVE AND DEPRAVED! In

other words hypocritical, toothless and ineffective in the United States and around the world—getting wealthy without taxation.

Politicians and lawyers

WHAT WOULD Y'SHUA THE MESSIAH SAY TO MOST OF OUR POLITICIANS AND LAWYERS? LIAR LIAR LIAR. DECEPTIVE DIVISIVE AND DEPRAVED—accomplishing nothing for Americans and citizens of the planet.

Business men and women

WHAT WOULD Y'SHUA THE MESSIAH SAY ABOUT MOST BUSINESS MEN AND WOMEN WHO ARE NOT ON WALL STREET? MONEY DRIVEN WITH NO HIGHER PURPOSE, IN IT FOR THEMSELVES AND GREEDY! Slave drivers underpaying Americans into servitude—accomplishing nothing for Americans and citizens of the planet.

Wall Street tycoons

WHAT WOULD Y'SHUA THE MESSIAH SAY ABOUT MOST WALL STREET TYCOONS? THIEVES WHO ARE DECEPTIVE, DRIVEN BY FEAR OF LOSING MONEY AND GREED WITHOUT HIGHER PURPOSE! American wealth and pension destroyers who steal from unsuspecting small time investors for their greedy fat pockets—accomplishing nothing for Americans and citizens of the planet.

<u>Judges</u>

WHAT WOULD Y'SHUA THE MESSIAH SAY ABOUT <u>MOST</u> JUDGES? LIARS LIARS LIARS. PRETENDING TO BE UPHOLDERS OF THE LAWS AND CONSTITUTION OF THE UNITED STATES, VIOLATORS OF GOD'S PURE JUSTICE, DELIVERING JUSTICE FOR ALL THE RICH AND POWERFUL AND INJUSTICE FOR THE MIDDLE AND POOR CLASSES OF ALL RACES, ESPECIALLY BLACK PEOPLE, OPERATING A DYSFUNCTIONAL JUSTICE AND LEGISLATION SYSTEM—American family destroyers who allow convictions on perjurious testimony freeing murderers and sending the innocent to jail—fathers of INJUSTICE—accomplishing nothing for Americans and citizens of the planet.

Above commentary is a sad state of affairs in the USA and around the world, but those comments about most spiritual and political leaders, lawyers, business men and women, Wall Street tycoons and judges are truths which explain why society is dysfunctional.

If **all of you** agree with me, which I know you do, it is not a coincidence that you are reading this today. When I say **all of you** I am including leadership of all parties—Democrats, Republicans and Tea Partiers unless the leadership is so confused and self-possessed that they are out of touch with reality, which would be the reason for new leadership—unadulterated with the games of politics and a dysfunctional legislative system. The new breed of leadership cannot come from those in Washington D.C. or professional lawyers and politicians, it has to be those whose goals and objectives are tailored to community and reaching across the walls that divide us as a people of this nation and the planet.

America must lead in this global revolution and I am here to say categorically that I was ordained for such a time as this based on my background and nothing else.

At this time, it doesn't matter what party you belong to. I am calling on Occupy Wall Street revolutionaries, Tea Partiers, Democrats, Republicans, all religious backgrounds, all races, ethnicities, languages, nationalities and sexual orientations to join me in this national and global revolution. We will never be perfect people, all of us, as long as our station is on Planet Earth, but we can strive after excellence—God's excellence in all areas of life.

CHAPTER 1

AM I REINCARNATED BASED ON MY NAMES?

As indicated earlier, friends, my name is Ronex James John Kennedy Muteshael. I was born in Zambia, Africa on April 7, 1959, a Good Friday—1 year and 7 months before the late beloved ex-president John Fitzgerald Kennedy (JFK) was elected president in November of 1960.

JFK's life was abruptly and mercilessly taken, as we all know, by assassination on November 22nd of 1963—4 years and 7 months after I was born. In my book "Unlocking Higher Performance: Learning From 24-7 Smart Billionaires and Millionaires™" I explain how I got my middle names John Kennedy.

Yes, I know what you are thinking and were thinking when I said my name is Ronex James John Kennedy Muteshael.

Depending on your spiritual belief system, you will have an explanation for what I am going to discuss—especially if you are Hebrew, Jewish, Christian, Buddhist, Hindu or you believe in reincarnation or believe in psychic or medium phenomenon, etc.

I found explanations for my unexplainable supernatural phenomenal events of my life in the Hebrew Scriptures of the Holy Bible. People say there are no coincidences in life. I agree. Absolutely true.

At my age of 52 years, the Almighty God, who was revealed by His Son Y'shua the Messiah has proved to me that He is really involved in our lives individually, nationally and globally.

Some of you may not understand what I will be discussing—please read the Bible and ask God to reveal His truth to you.

Based on my names, Ronex James John Kennedy Muteshael and my personal unexplainable experiences some people have told me that I am reincarnated John Fitzgerald Kennedy, Ronald Wilson Reagan and Jesus Christ.

In Zambia as well as the United States my legal names were and have been Ronex Kennedy Mutesha. However, when I came to the United States, even though my legal names were Ronex Kennedy Mutesha, I truncated my names to Ron K. Mutesha. Because most people would ask me what the "K" stood for, I decided to truncate my name further to Ron Mutesha or Ronex Mutesha.

I have given a few reasons why I chose to do that in my book mentioned above. The most glaring reason is that I did not want to draw attention to myself or the Kennedys for that matter. I wanted to avoid possible speculation, controversy and even scandal mongering by the media. Though on my website and in my book I say neither JFK nor the other Kennedys had anything to do with my names—my family never told me that, I just guessed from the way I was named as I explain in my book.

I have a detailed explanation of my unexplainable personal experiences and my take on the issue in my books **Ronex James *John Kennedy* Mute*Shael's Glo*bal *R*evolution—Awakening the USA to its authentic global leadership role!"** and my current book "Unlocking Higher Performance—Learning from 24/7 Smart Billionaires and Millionaires™." Please visit my website at www.RonexOnline.com for my plan of action to secure the future of the USA and the planet for all our children on the planet.

In 2003 at the age of 44, between April 7th, 2003 (my birthday) and May 29, 2003 (JFK's birthday) for what I call divine reasons I decided to start using my full legal names—Ronex Kennedy Mutesha.

And beginning January 7, 2009 I decided to use my full set of names I was given on April 7th, 1959. In my book I give reasons why I did that.

It is not a coincidence, but that Almighty God had divine purpose for my life based on the names I was given and my last name Mutesha(el). I have no doubt whatsoever.

Just to give you examples of what people have conjured up each time I disclosed my full set of names, it has been all as I anticipated.

Between April 7th, 2003 (My birth day when I turned age **44**) and May 29th, 2003 (JFK'S birthday) I had experienced a phenomenon I had never before. The best way to describe this is what you read in Acts Chapter Two of the Bible when the disciples of **JESUS CHRIST** were waiting for the **HOLY SPIRIT** to anoint them.

"WHOOOOOOSH," like a mighty wind rushing into my whole body—except, I was in my bedroom with windows closed. "Where did that wind come from?" I asked myself. After this incident, within this time frame, I was given a vision, which I eventually labeled prophecy, that **President #44 of these United States of America will be a Black man**.

Barack Obama was elected president of the United States in November of 2008 five years later. I was declared insane and delusional for saying **President #44 of these United States of America will be a Black man.** I was vindicated by the LORD.

During this period I was actually in and out of what you call experiential visions during the day and at night. Right around JFK's birthday May 29th, 2003 at my age of 44, the same age of 44 at which JFK became president of the United States, I visionary experienced JFK's presidency as though I was there, being him—sort of like in a trance.

Around June **4th** or the **5th** of 2003 I also visionary experienced Ronald Wilson Reagan's presidency as though I was there, being him---sort of like in a trance again. Those were strange kind's of experiences I had never been through before. What is amazing about this is that almost to the exact date, a year later, Ronald Wilson Reagan died on June 5th, 2004.

Sometime between **April 7th, 2003 and December 5th, 2003,** I went through a visionary tour of the past going back to the time of Y'shua the Messiah, His birth and crucifixion to future events in my life, some of which have already taken place.

After being declared insane and delusional for saying **President #44 of these United States of America will be a Black man,** one of the four times when my ex-wife called paramedics on me I ended up at Elgin Mental Health Center (EMHC) and my interaction with a particular Hispanic lady who was also admitted at EMHC was mind boggling to me.

When I saw her the first time, she was one of those cases where she would pee in her pants. That's what got my attention. Each time she made eye contact with me she would stare at me. I went up to her, smiled and said, "Hi." She never said hi back other than just stare at me. I didn't know what was going on in her mind, obviously. When we finally did this about three times, she asked me if I was there to put her in jail. I said, "no, I am not here to do that."

The next time we made eye contact, I walked up to her to say hi. Before I could say hi, she asked me a question, "Are you Jesus Christ?" I smiled and said, "No, but I know Jesus Christ." I don't know what made her ask or what she saw for her to ask me the question. Friends, I am Black, there is no way I was expecting someone to mistake me for Y'shua the Christ (delusional or not, mentally ill or not) based on the portraits of Y'shua the Christ we have seen—a blue eyed Caucasian and for sure English. Obviously she was ill, no doubt about that, from her behavior, but her question totally amazed me. I didn't know what to make of it other than believe, later, that this was one more thing the Lord had to do to make sure I never ever doubt that I am His follower. The other aspect about this is, "Was this question, "Are you Jesus Christ?" confirming the likely visitation by Y'shua the Christ?" Did she see a vision of Y'shua the Christ, somehow? I have asked myself these questions many times. My conclusion is a resounding YES.

In John 14:19-20 (NKJV) the Christ tells His disciples and I quote:

"A little while longer and *the world will see Me no more*, but *you will see Me*. Because I live, *you will live also*. At that day you will know that *I am in My Father, and you in Me, and I in you.*

Confirmed by the Bible as stated above. The Hispanic lady saw the Christ alive in me. I prayed for this lady and in two days of my interaction with her, including giving her a hug, she was transformed. She combed her hair, looked gorgeous, was smiling and I didn't see any more incidences I described above. She no longer seemed like she was out of it. Not a coincidence at all.

During this same period, my ex-wife had asked me the same question. It was right after we turned off lights in our bedroom that I decided to bring up marital issues. I like referencing the Bible as my guide in addressing some issues. As I talked in the dark, my ex-wife responded with a question to what I said with a strange kind of voice—not her usual voice saying, "Are you Jesus Christ?" I didn't respond to the question other than shutting my mouth, stopped talking and went to sleep wondering what that was all about.

My take on this is that the Spirit of God allowed me to experience these lives to get a deeper understanding of visions God had assigned to them to pass them on to me—JFK's, RWR's, and the Lord Y'shua's. That is how I concluded my assignment on Planet Earth was defined through the names I was given and adopted on April 7th, 1959 which was a Good Friday.

Have I ever wished I was the Christ so I can propel the good works He started? Of course!

Have I ever wished I was JFK and RWR so I can continue from where they left off? Of course!

What happened in the above scenario is similar to what takes place between **El-i-jah** and **El-i-sha** in 2 Kings 2:9-12(NKJV) (**El**, **Jah** and **Sha** are all Hebrew references to God (or names of God). Notice my name—Mute-**sha**-**el**. God heard my private wishes. Here is the passage of Scripture and I quote:

> "And so it was, when they had crossed over, that Elijah said to Elisha, "Ask! What may I do for you, before I am taken away from you?" Elisha said, "***Please let a double portion of your spirit be upon me.***" So he said, "You have asked a hard thing. *Nevertheless,* if you see me *when I am* taken from you, it shall be so for you; but if not, it shall not be *so.*" Then it happened, as they continued on and talked, that suddenly a chariot of fire *appeared* with horses of fire, and separated the two of them; and Elijah went up by a whirlwind into heaven. And Elisha saw *it*, and he cried out, "My father, my father, the chariot of Israel and its horsemen!" So he saw him no more."

The above is a transference of God's spirit which was on El-i-jah onto El-i-sha. Elijah did not reincarnate into Eli-sha. Transference of God's spirit from one individual to another is what we call anointing the receiver with the legacy or calling or mission or leadership ability. Again the Bible provides the answer explaining my experiences. My experiences are validated by scripture. God has not changed in the way He operates.

In verses 13 through 15 of 2 Kings chapter 2 (NKJV), it says and I quote:

> "He also took up ***the mantle of Elijah*** that had fallen from him, and went back and stood by the bank of the Jordan. Then he took the mantle of Elijah that had fallen from him, and struck the water, and said, "***Where is the Lord God of Elijah?***" And when he also had struck the water, ***it was divided this way and that***; and Elisha crossed over. Now when the sons of the prophets who *were* from Jericho saw him, they said, ***"The spirit of Elijah rests on Elisha."*** And they came to meet him, and bowed to the ground before him."

My ex-wife since 2003 told others including psychologists and psychiatrists that I was behaving like a president though I did not personally claim to be one.

There is a difference between thinking that you are somebody else and having a vision of becoming President of the United States or Zambia for that matter.

Visions I had were confirming the transference of the Spirit of God for leadership that were on JFK, RWR and yes the Lord Y'shua the Christ.

Real leadership comes through God anointing that person. And all God appointed kings were prophetic in their lives.

The anointing of king Saul resulted in prophetic utterances as recorded in 1 Samuel 10:6-7,9-10 (NKJV) and I quote:

> "Then the Spirit of the Lord will come upon you, and **you will prophesy** with them and be **turned into another man**. And let it be, when these signs come to you, *that* you do as the occasion demands; for **God *is* with you**……So it was, when he had turned his back to go from Samuel, that God gave him another heart; and all **those signs came to pass** that day. When they came there to the hill, there was a group of prophets to meet him; then the Spirit of God came upon him, and he prophesied among them."

In the same way the anointing of king David resulted in prophetic utterances through out his life. In 1 Samuel 16:13 (NKJV) it says and I quote:

> "And the Lord said, "Arise, **anoint him; for this *is* the one**!" Then Samuel took the horn of oil and anointed him in the midst of his brothers; and the **Spirit of the Lord came upon David** from that day forward."

The most important prophetic utterance king David makes is about the coming Savior and Messiah and the crucifixion of Him—the Lord Y'shua in Psalm 22:16-18 (NKJV) and I quote:

> "For dogs have surrounded Me; The congregation of the wicked has enclosed Me. **They pierced My hands and My feet**; I can count all My bones. They look *and* stare at Me. They divide My garments among them, And for My clothing they cast lots."

King David predicted the coming of the King of kings. God, through me, predicted the coming of the 44th president of the USA, Barack Obama, who was compared to some kind of a messiah and some compared him to JFK. I did not consider Barack as any of that though I saw his coming on the scene.

On the other hand I am Ronex James **John Kennedy** Mute*Shael*, I share two names with **John** Fitzgerald **Kennedy** and my last name is one of God's Hebrew names (***Shael***) and my last name decoded becomes a prophet's name and reversed describes the characteristic of the Messiah—***Almighty(El) God (Sha)*-Man**.

I have no doubt Barack was meant to be the 44th president of the USA, but that he was a fore-shadowing of real unmistakable anointed leadership the United States needs at this time, and everything that I am speaks to that. All you have to do is look at the background of everyone running for the office of the president—they are far from matching mine. I have a documented short and long range plan of action on fixing what is wrong in the United States—they don't have a plan. Who would you go with based on what I have said so far? Coincidence? Absolutely not!

America is God's country. I strongly believe so. So is every nation on the planet. But I believe that God had an authentic divine global leadership role for the USA, but our leadership has failed to ascend to that role because of the Constitution of the United States.

God desires that leaders be anointed, prophetic and obedient to His word---be truth tellers. Not to proclaim peace when there is no peace, but to rebuke and correct to repentance so nations can inherit God's blessings—spiritual and yes peace and prosperity.

Why has the United States become dysfunctional to the highest degree? The answer to that is found in Hosea 8:4 (NKJV) and I quote:

> "They set up kings, but ***not by Me***; They made princes, but I ***did not acknowledge them***. From their ***silver and gold*** They made idols for themselves—

After 44 presidential administrations, the USA is broke and dysfunctional. Our system of government has clearly with certainty not worked for all Americans as it has been clearly communicated through the 99% and results are proof in the pudding.

Most of our presidents were not and have not been set-up and acknowledged by God as Hosea the prophet states. Barack has served his purpose of communicating a past and the immediate future. Based on all the above and everything else I discuss herein and other material I have put together, Rick Perry, Mitt Romney, Michele Bachmann, Hermann Cain, Newt Gingrich and anybody else were not meant to be president # 45.

I can assure you that without the plan of action I have outlined, for which I boldly state that I was ordained to implement, the USA will sink deeper into its self-inflicted dysfunction because it is the same two parties that are responsible for the dysfunction—same archaic ideas that only work for the rich and powerful and the leadership of both parties, not the 99%. PERIOD. What's new? Zilch.

I refer to what I am all about as God foretelling my future through my names, education, and real life personal, industry and business experiences—and of course spiritual, supernatural and unexplainable experiences I have gone through. But, was God also telling me about my prior life existence to my current life as in being reincarnated?

A twenty something friend of mine by the name of Cliff Powers, who studies dreams/visions and the supernatural said that what I experienced was reincarnation. I don't believe in reincarnation, but I believe in the incarnation of Y'shua the Christ as God-Man.

Can good human spirits (JFK and RWR) influence other human beings like evil spirits do when allowed by the subject or God Almighty Himself allows it? If the answer to that question is yes and some people call it reincarnation, maybe they are right. Am I reincarnated JFK or RWR or Y'shua the Christ Himself? I prefer to say, I am Ronex James John Kennedy Muteshael. Why do I say that? I say that because I am not really like JFK, RWR or Y'shua the Christ, though I know for sure that Y'shua the Christ is the infinitely overwhelming influence in my life who is infinitely capable of anything. My role today at the national and global level was fore-ordained by the Almighty and I will not shrink from that conclusion based on the word of God.

Read my book, Unlocking Higher Performance—Learning from 24/7 Smart Billionaires & Millionaires™ for more of my life experiences.

The question is: How can I have those experiences which are exactly related to those I call my top three mentors? People talk about transference of spirit. When we say, "He/she has the spirit of so and so," is that referring to the concept of reincarnation? You answer that. But, that's what happened to me. Based on the above Biblical explanation I am not "reincarnated-anybody." Do you understand what I am saying? Yes, I bet you do.

Summary of predictions that came to pass and are unfolding

- JFK was 44 years old when he became president in 1961. I was 44 years old when, by the grace of God I predicted that president #44 of the United States was going to be a Black man.
- In 2003 at the age of 44 is when I embarked upon my global mission www.RonexOnline.Com.: The Ronex James John Kennedy Muteshael—24/7 SmartGROUPNetwork™.
- I was born on April 7, 1959, a Good Friday—1 year and 7 months before JFK was elected president in November of 1960. From my name Muteshael you derive el-sha-thu-me which means Y'shua the Messiah who was crucified on Good Friday. My names John Kennedy were prophetic as to who would be the next president of the United States in 1 year and 7 months at that time in 1959.
- Without thinking about it, I registered my domain name RonexOnline.Com on April 7, 2011 exactly 1 year and 7 months before the November 2012 presidential election. If America is in tune with God's providence to solutions we need today and His generational involvement in affairs of nations, my names, Ronex James John Kennedy Muteshael, are once again, prophetic as to who should be the next president of the United States 1 year and 7 months from April 7, 2011—president #45. America has free agency—to accept or reject God's provision, and therefore accept results that come with that freedom to choose.
- When between April 7th, 2003 and May 29th, 2003, I predicted that **President #44 of these United States will be a Black man,** people didn't believe me—including my own family. My now 14 year old son, Zeke, recalled the prediction in the presence of my friend George Isaacson. This prediction was before I knew anything about Mr. Barack Obama and it was before his speech at the DNC of 2004. A prediction against a backdrop that John Kerry was running to become president #44.
- The above prediction was divine in nature in that between December 4th and 5th of 2003 by the grace of God, I predicted that *Mr. George W. Bush, president #43 would get a second term in office*. Political pundits said George W. would be a one term president like his father. Both the re-election and election of George W. and Barack respectively *were historical*.
- I predicted a national and global revolution to fix dysfunction in the U.S. and around the world in April of 2011. In July of 2011 Occupy Wall Street was initiated by a consumer advocate in Canada. That revolution, is in line with what I declared in 2001-2003 about helping the 99% of society.

Imagine the chances of above predictions coming true against all odds *within 8 years*— predictions made between April of 2003 and April 2011. As indicated, both the re-election and election of George W. and Barack respectively *were historical*.

There is **no prophet** alive today that I am aware of that may have predicted as accurately as I did with immediate confirmation of above critical events in the life of the United States and the planet as a whole. The number 44 was the confirmation that made me realize the visions were from the Almighty and therefore they were going to come true. If nobody has predicted or did predict the above and either way, I am humbled that Almighty God chose to disclose this crucial information to me authenticating the anointing. It was not a coincidence that my family gave me as middle names John Kennedy—names of a legendary president JFK. My names were prophetic as to who was going to be president in 1960 and at the exact same age of 44 at which JFK became president the Almighty would give me a prophecy about president #44. There is no way my parents and I would have orchestrated this. God did. PERIOD!

The essence of a prophetic utterance sometimes is to warn about pending catastrophes so we can take certain courses of action, to avoid, especially so, loss of life or economic destructive events, hence my declaration of those courses of action herein and my other materials.

Each time I tell people my full names, they automatically think that I am related to the Kennedys; and the topic of running for the presidency of the USA and whether or not I am related to the Kennedys always comes up.

When I jokingly said to a twenty something Caucasian friend of mine, Paul David Olsson, that I am going to run for the presidency, he said that I could not because of the U.S. Constitution since I wasn't born here. When I jokingly said, "f— the Constitution," which is what judges in Lake County, Cook County, DuPage County and Kane County are doing, he jokingly responded saying, "You must be JFK's illegitimate son the Kennedys left to run the country." We burst out laughing. Now you understand why I didn't use my full names.

When I was in jail a Caucasian fellow inmate by the name of James Turuc(sic), at Lake County Jail in Waukegan, Illinois, at one time asked me about what I was working on, on the computer, I said, "I am writing a book." "What is it about?," he asked. I briefly explained what it was all about. "What's the title?," he asked. When I told him the title, he exclaimed, "You are John "f expletive" Kennedy!!" We laughed. He and I were what they call "POD attorneys" assisting fellow inmates with their legal issues and constructing legal motions for them.

At another time a sixty something Caucasian friend of mine, George Isaacson, responded almost the same way when I revealed my full names to him. He said, "I didn't know the Kennedys were in Africa too." And added that, "You should find out a little more about your ancestry." I just laughed.

A psychiatrist, by the name of Dr. Chandra, who probably believes in reincarnation, came up with another fib saying that I was JFK who reincarnated into a Black man's skin so he could see how he would be treated as a Black man. If this psychiatrist was right, I am here to tell you that the Black JFK was discriminated against and mistreated in almost all circles of interaction.

IPA's paralegal, Amy K. Chase, in her affidavit lied saying that I claimed to be a reincarnated JFK and also that I was claiming to be JFK risen from the grave.

Some friends of mine, who know my middle names as John Kennedy have jokingly called me JFK. And yes I have jokingly kidded about it to get a laugh—some people don't get the joke. Seriously, lawyers, psychiatrists/ psychologists and some people who don't get the joke, have thought I am delusional or insane.

Friends for the record—my names are Ronex James John Kennedy Muteshael or RJJKM. I am not JFK, neither am I Ronald W. Reagan. I have never been insane and I am not insane. I love to laugh and enjoy a good joke.

For those of you who sincerely believe that I am reincarnated JFK, RWR and Y'shua the Messiah, I must apologize that I didn't come back sooner to fix the dysfunctions we face today in the United States and as God's global community. Did you get the joke? It may be a joke, but I strongly believe that I was meant to come to the aid of the United States and our planet at such a time as this.

CHAPTER 2

**MY 24/7 SMART PERFORMANCE IMPROVEMENT TOOLS TO CARRY OUT THE MISSION/OBJECTIVE
At the Individual, Corporate, National & Global Level
Total Action Plan (TAP) ("Operation TAP")**

In 2001, soon after 9/11, after realizing the direction in which our country, these United States, was headed—into the bliss of dysfunction in all essential aspects of life, I decided to do something about it. The result is a set of PERFORMANCE IMPROVEMENT TOOLS and my website:

www.RonexOnline.Com
The Ronex James John Kennedy Muteshael
24/7 SmartG.R.O.U.P.Network™.

The Performance Handbook: Unlocking Higher Performance—Learning From 24/7 Smart Billionaires & Millionaires™ is part summary of my life experiences which brought me to where I am today.

To understand the concept behind the 24-7 Smart System of Strategies visit RJJKM Online Store to purchase the system, use it and I guarantee improvement in your performance in all essential areas of life regardless of your profession, industry or personal belief system.

In short a 24/7 Smart Billionaire or Millionaire is a person who does business God's way. I was inspired to create these tools to empower the 99% of the United States and the planet for their total freedom—financial and in all other areas, the cornerstone being our spiritual aspect of life:

Spiritual freedom for all,
Judicial freedom for all,
Political freedom for all,
Educational freedom for all,
Financial freedom for all,
Economical freedom for all and
Social freedom for all.

Briefly here are descriptions of what you can find in the "24-7 SMART SYSTEM OF STRATEGIES" PERFORMANCE IMPROVEMENT TOOLS:

1. The Performance Handbook: Unlocking Higher Performance—Learning From 24/7 Smart Billionaires & Millionaires™
—ISBN 978-1-257-65789-6
2. Unlocking Higher Performance : The 24/7 Smart Master Planner™
—ISBN 978-1-257-65786-5
3. Unlocking Higher Performance : The 24/7 Smart Planner & Journal System™
—ISBN 978-1-257-65787-2
4. Unlocking Higher Performance : The 24/7 Smart Daily Personal Money Tracker System™
—ISBN 978-1-257-65441-3

1. The Performance Handbook: Unlocking Higher Performance
   Learning From 24/7 Smart Billionaires & Millionaires™
   - The book will first of all help you *find your mission or calling* in this life and *liberate the spirit of enterprise* in you. This is so you will be doing what you were meant to do in this life.
   - Finding your mission will *create a passion* for what you were meant to do — your mission in this life.
   - Then the book will direct you in how to *get organized* on an individual basis and as a business or non-profit organization to pursue your mission.
   - The book will also show you how you can dramatically *unlock higher (or improve) performance* in all essential areas of your life—business/job as well as personal: the total *Personal and Business Plan*.
   - Liberating the spirit of enterprise in individuals will result *in the creation and building of businesses and non-profit organizations*.
   - Building of businesses and non-profit organizations will result in the *creation of jobs* which helps the economy.
   - Includes my prophetic visions of:
     —the 2nd Term Office of USA President # 43
     —USA President #44
     —My Assignment:www.RonexOnline.Com
     —USA President # 45

At this point you can guess who I believe and know should be president #45. Some dysfunctions, especially ones we face today, can only be dealt with by those who were ordained for such tasks. And this I promise you that, without choosing the right leadership today, I am certain based on the word of God that America will descend further into this morass of confusion and despondency.

2. Unlocking Higher Performance : The 24/7 Smart Master Planner™
   - The *24/7 Smart Master Planner™* helps you get organized on an individual basis and/or as a business or non-profit organization to pursue your mission.
   - The *24/7 Smart Master Planner™* further facilitates *unlocking higher performance dramatically* in all essential areas of life—at your job or business and on a personal level (including your spiritual life); it is your *Total Personal and Business Plan.*
   - Ultimately it helps you cater to what matters and that is why it works.

3. Unlocking Higher Performance : The 24/7 Smart Planner & Journal System™
   - Based on the *Master Planner* this *24/7 Smart Planner and Journal System™* helps you do *minute by minute, hourly, daily, weekly, monthly, yearly, short-term and long-term planning and execution* as you pursue your mission.
   - Since you know where you want/need to be in 5 years, for instance, the *24/7 Smart Planner and Journal System™* will help break down your bigger goals into smaller manageable ones that will assuredly lead you to achieving your ultimate goals.
   - The *24/7 Smart Planner and Journal System™* also, through journal pages, helps you reflect on your day and contemplate the future. Write it all down, you never know. Everything starts from a thought that may develop into *something big. By combining the planner and journal, it makes it easier to transfer ideas you come up with in your journaling into an action item for your planner.*

4. Unlocking Higher Performance : The 24/7 Smart Daily Personal Money Tracker System™
   - Are you one of those people who *writes checks against your checking account without knowing how much money you have in the account?*
   - If you have *a lot of money* in it and your withdrawals are minute compared to what you have in the account, you may have *no overdraft problems and other charges.*
   - If you *don't have a lot of money* you may end up with an account that is *overdrawn with a lot of bank fees that eat up your money.*
   - You need to keep track of your *daily money activities* in your checking account. Not only does your *24-7 Smart Daily Personal Money Tracker System™* help you track your money activities in your *checking account*, it helps you keep track of your *piggy bank, cash on hand* (in your *pocket and wallet*), *savings, child support* and

other (*money market, business,* etc.) money activities.
- And then the *24-7 Smart Daily Personal Money Tracker System*™ helps you summarize your *total money* that day. Know how much money (*to the penny*) you have on a daily basis using this tool the *24-7 Smart Daily Personal Money Tracker System*™.

In the United States we all can use above resources and especially so the U.S. government to keep track of its income and expenditures to avert a budget deficit. Is it a coincidence that I was inspired to create these resources to help everyone in the US including the US government and yes other peoples and nations? No it was by divine inspiration—it was purposed.

Friends, <u>**no candidate in the U.S.**</u> has ever laid out a plan of action such as I have based on education, industry and business experience, but above all, that if we are going to contend that we are a Christian Nation, then lets emulate Y'shua in the way we act in all essential aspects of life—love of God and love of others as ourselves—helping people help themselves—the top 1% comprehending the plight of the 99%. Mine is a perfect plan that works for all. IT CAN BE DONE!

CHAPTER 3

MY OBJECTIVE/MISSION

The Ronex James John Kennedy Muteshael—24/7 SmartG.R.O.U.P. Network™ is dedicated to providing and facilitating procurement of products, services and resources for the development of individuals, small and medium size businesses, non-profit and faith-based organizations across the U.S.A. and the world at large, with the objective of helping people pursue their God-given mission on the planet and to create jobs.

Friends, the USA is dysfunctional because our leaders are not driven by higher purpose—they have no God-given mission of helping people help themselves. The presidency is about how they can use it for themselves and their partial local interest—not all Americans and they don't care about the plight of those suffering from mass misery around the world. The truth is no human being or nation is invincible to tragedies fashioned by the Creator Himself, even superpowers and cash-cows of today. Technology has not saved us from bankruptcy and all dysfunctions that exist today. That is fact.

Rick Perry, Mitt Romney, Michele Bachmann, Herman Cain, Newt Gingrich and Barack Obama have no credible plans, leaders from the same parties with values that are responsible for where we are TODAY. It doesn't matter who is or who is going to be in office from these parties, it is the same old. Net accomplishments? NEGATIVE AND TOTALLY IRRESPONSIBLE.

Diverse And Striving For An Integrated Nation And Global Community

The United States of America is a nation of people from all walks life, various countries, races, ethnicities, religious persuasions, languages, colors, nationalities, men and women, young and young at heart, sexual orientations, etc. The entire human race is represented in these United States. I love you all, regardless of who you are, with the unconditional love of the Almighty Himself and yes Y'shua the Messiah. We can no longer be *separate but equal* as separation promotes unequal distribution of resources creating unleveled playing fields resulting in some citizens depending on the government for sustenance.

How long is too long or is it too soon that we need time for real integration and unity as a people of this nation and Planet Earth? Or are we waiting like our founding fathers for another Civil War or uprisings as we have witnessed in Europe and now in the USA? Time is not on our side.

Already doing what the president of the USA is supposed to do

Through my website, RonexOnline.Com—the Ronex James John Kennedy Muteshael—24/7 SmartG.R.O.U.P.Network™, I am already doing what the president of the USA is supposed to do. Because I am reaching out to everyone on the planet I am in essence doing what presidents of every nation must be doing to eliminate the world wide economic and financial melt down.

Blessed With Visionary Leadership Ability

I thank the Almighty for blessing me with prophetic visionary leadership ability to be able to predict what would happen in the future authenticating my leadership role I was meant to play at the national and global level.

Based on what the Bible teaches who would you say was ordained to lead our global community for the betterment of our global community today? RJJKM!

The USA is a complex system of endeavors

As I say, the USA and the rest of the planet for that matter combined is a complex system of individual, national and global endeavors. Figuring out how it has worked in the past and how it works today and determining what is dysfunctional to brainstorm solutions, the president, of especially the USA, needs to be adequately familiar with how all essential aspects of life interact through real life industry experience and education. He needs to know how to provide a conducive environment for business start-ups and development, and nurturing those already in existence—small, mid-size or large to perpetuate job creation, continuous quality and productivity improvement. Non-profits and faith based organization involved in human outreach projects must also be nurtured for it is through these that we all can express our values of faith, family, courage and love.

Review of our 235 years of being a nation has made me conclude based on our circumstances today that lawyers and politicians are ill-equipped in terms of education and appropriate industry and business management experience to understand a complex structure such as the world in which we live today. They do not comprehend the big picture because they are focused on their partial local and constituent interests—hence our political dysfunction among other things.

My extensive education background to Ph.D. level, extensive industrial and business management experience, my action and results oriented performance in industry among other things sets me apart from every president that has ever been elected to the presidency of the USA—in fact on the whole planet.

All contenders for the presidency of the United States for 2012 are far removed from being a match to my background. Coincidence? The LORD

Yahweh guided my steps through education, industry and other personal experiences to bring me up for this complicated task before this nation and the planet. I had little to do with it—read my book and I certainly know you will agree with me.

CHAPTER 4

PROPHETIC DESTINY OF THE USA UTTERED BY BENJAMIN FRANKLIN
AT THE U.S. CONSTITUTION CONVENTION

To understand what is going on today, we need to go back to the beginning—the beginning of the United States and all the way to Genesis.

I am going to talk about Benjamin Franklin, and I am not here to discuss his affairs with French women, but what he said on June 28, 1787 at the Constitution Convention of the United States. Benjamin Franklin said and I quote,

"I have lived, Sir, a long time, and the longer I live, the more convincing proof I see of **this truth—that God governs in the affairs of men.** And if a sparrow cannot fall to the ground without his notice, **is it probable that an empire can rise without his aid**? We have been assured, Sir, in the sacred writings, that "**except the Lord build the House**, they labor in vain that build it." I firmly believe this; and I also believe that without **his concurring aid we shall succeed in this political building no better, than the Builders of Babel**. We shall be **divided by our partial local interests**; our projects will be **confounded**, and we ourselves shall become **a reproach and bye word down to future ages**. And what is worse, mankind may hereafter from this unfortunate instance, despair of establishing Governments by **Human wisdom** and leave it to **chance**, **war** and **conquest**. I therefore beg leave to move—that henceforth prayers **imploring the assistance of Heaven**, and **its blessings on our deliberations**, be held in this Assembly every morning before we proceed to business, and that one or more of the clergy of this city be requested to officiate in that service."

Parker Hudson, writes, in his book, "The President," and I quote **"Contrary to popular belief, our Founding Fathers fully intended to build a nation that was based on God's enduring principles. Based on the health of our political system today, Benjamin Franklin's warning against any other course of action seems eerily prophetic."**

I partially agree with Parker Hudson. The reason why I partially agree with Parker is because, yes, Benjamin Franklin would have wanted to build the United States **based on God's enduring principles.**

However, when the Constitution of the United States was drafted wherein they declared that White women and Africans were 3/5th of a person, it goes without saying that that declaration as legal as it was based on the Constitution was illegal based on the teachings of not only Biblical Hebrew Scriptures but the teachings of Y'shua the Messiah.

We condemn slavery today in the strongest terms where ever it is taking place on the planet and without compromise we stand for voting rights for women. Therefore the Constitution as drafted predetermined the dysfunctions we see today.

How can you declare, in the same mouth, "all men were created equal" in 1776 and eleven years later in 1787 change your tune. It is what I am calling and Christ would call hypocrisy. Unfortunately that mentality and hypocrisy still exists today to a great extent here in the United States—the rise of the 99% who are considered not equal to the top 1% is a great example of this inequality.

I am here to say we are living this prophecy by Benjamin Franklin, right now. Nobody can stop this prophecy other than the LORD. Think about all that is going in this country. We are **confounded.** Borrowing money from countries that don't respect human rights? When we do what we are doing, aren't we being a **reproach and by-word**? **Eerily prophetic!!**

Remember that Benjamin Franklin was one of 57 people that signed the declaration of independence and one of 39 people that signed the Constitution of the United States wherein they declared that White women and Africans were 3/5th of a person. If in fact Benjamin signed the Constitution of the United States, was he serious about his statement? And if in fact prayers were uttered **imploring the assistance of Heaven**, and **its blessings on the deliberations**, and they drafted a constitution that discriminated against White women, Africans, Native Americans and other ethnicities, from which **Heaven did they implore assistance** every morning before they proceeded to business?

Further more our founding fathers did not consider some Whites as equals, for example the Irish. You find this prejudice in hiring practices where employment ads would say, "Irish may not apply."

George Washington, the presiding officer of the U.S. Constitution Convention, at that time was a slave master. Therefore it was in his ***personal agenda*** to legalize slavery and criminalize freedom of slaves. Not only did George Washington own African slaves, he had Caucasian indentured servants who were subject to involuntary servitude, that is, cheap Caucasian labor. What has changed? Nothing. The top 1% own the 99% as slaves.

CHAPTER 5

PROOF POSITIVE THAT THE U.S. CONSTITUTION HAS FAILED TO WORK FOR ORDINARY AMERICANS
—THE 14 FACTORS—

Today, here in the USA we need to ask ourselves the following questions and give truthful answers without political spinning for that is the only way we can determine root causes of problems we find today:

1. Did the United States rise without God's aid? No. God was involved.
2. Have our leaders of these United States from 1776 till today allowed the Lord to build our Nation as Benjamin suggested? The answer is NO.
3. Based on the political atmosphere in Washington D.C. are we divided by our partial local interests? The answer is Yes—we have conservatives, liberals, moderates and independents.
4. Based on what is going on in Washington D.C. wouldn't you say our leaders are confounded meaning confused? Yes they are.
5. Wouldn't you say, based on where we are today, that we, as the United States, have become a reproach and bye word in this age as predicted by Benjamin Franklin, especially that we are borrowing money from China, whose leaders have no respect for human rights? Yes we have.
6. Has the justice system worked for Americans of all races, the poor and the middle class? NO!
7. Has Wall Street worked for Americans of all races, the poor and the middle class? NO!
8. Has the legislative system worked for Americans of all races, the poor, the middle class and legitimate business owners? NO!
9. Have financial institutions worked for Americans of all races, the poor and the middle class? NO!
10. Have economic and infrastructure systems worked for Americans of all races, the poor and the middle class? NO!
11. Have social systems worked for Americans of all races and the poor? NO!
12. Has our foreign policy worked for the USA? No. We are creating more enemies than partners on the planet.
13. Has our human construed moral value system worked for Americans of all races, the poor, the middle class, and the rich and powerful? NO!
14. Has our spiritual belief system—Christianity yielded results we would

expect? No. If not, why not?

The above answers should tell any objective observer that we have dysfunction in all essential areas of life after being a nation for 235 years. Since our answers to all 14 questions imply dysfunction after being a nation for 235 years, what it means is that the dysfunctions were inbuilt and embedded into our systems by our founding fathers deliberately and through oversight.

What America and the world needs, as America is being emulated by various nations on the planet, is not reformation but re-founding.

When the founding fathers saw that the tyrannical system set in place by the British monarchy wasn't working for them, the American Revolutionary war ensued. Obviously we appreciate what the founding fathers attempted to create as the USA. However, it has not worked for every American.

My global revolution is not a declaration of war against other nations or a civil war within to put in place new systems that would work for every American and every human being on the planet, but one of logically reasoning with all Americans and all citizens of the planet to the fact that we need to re-found the USA and the planet so systems we put in place can work for all Americans and all citizens of the planet.

There is no other human being alive today that was raised for this complicated task of reengineering all essential systems of life so they work for all humanity—my life experiences up to this point have prepared me for such a time as this when the world needs someone like me.

I am driven by the passion of the Christ for all humanity within the USA and outside. The collective brain-trust, gifted to all of us by the Almighty as citizens of the planet, can brainstorm solutions to all issues we face today if we allow the unconditional love of God for all humanity to be our driving force and the basis on which we build all essentials systems of life in our global society.

There is a first for everything, like **_the first American president born outside the USA_**. I was raised for that and that is why my family appropriately named me and I ended up as Ronex James John Kennedy Muteshael (RJJKM).

CHAPTER 6

RJJKM'S GLOBAL REVOLUTION —AWAKENING THE USA TO ITS AUTHENTIC GLOBAL LEADERSHIP ROLE— THROUGH TOTAL FREEDOM INDEED REVOLUTION

I have all the education I need and then some. Above all I am a student of the Bible. It is time for these USA and the planet as a whole to experience foremost Total Freedom Indeed which will lead to all other freedoms—Real Judicial, Political, Educational, Financial, Economical and Social Freedom for all Americans—Black, Brown, Red, Yellow and White.

I have been here in the United States for 27 years, worked in almost all essential sectors of industry and assisted several companies and a non-profit improve their performance in various ways. All that pales compared to my experiences when I was forced into mental health institutions and I was recently arrested on September 9, 2008 on fabricated charges of spitting on a police officer after conducting my own version of *Occupy Wall Street* against International Profit Associates (IPA). Thank God I was released December 20, 2010. It was in jail that I got the vision I am calling the RJJKM'S Global Revolution—Awakening the USA to its authentic global leadership role through Total Freedom Indeed Revolution.

Born April 7th, 1959 which was a Good Friday and being named Ronex James *John Kennedy* Mutesha 1 year and 7 months before *John* Fitzgerald *Kennedy* was elected president of the United States in 1960 remained a mystery until 2003.

Before I proceed in this chapter, I want everybody reading this manifesto to know this that I love all peoples of the planet—Africans, Americans (North and South), Asians, Europeans, Middle Easterners, Australians, New Zealanders, all nations, all countries, all races, all ethnicities and all languages because God loves the world. He loves both sinners and saints. There is nothing more I would like to see than all nations working together to make the world a better and safer place for all our children.

In today's world we cannot talk about securing the United States outside of a global context. That, would be delusional, myopic and archaic. I desire so much that the United States awaken to its authentic global leadership role. Our leaders in the United States past and present have failed miserably to ascend to this God assigned endeavor of being an authentic global leader, hence the dysfunctions we see today in all essential areas of life within the United States and outside.

   As I have said, to understand what is going on today, we need to go back to the beginning—the beginning of the United States and all the way to Genesis as I indicated.

CHAPTER 7

MY MENTORS WITHIN THE CONTEXT OF MY NAMES
Ronex James *John Kennedy* Mute*shael* —The Mission Within

Briefly, the main reason why I decided to use my full names at birth, and adding an "el" to my last name is because my full names at birth defined my subsuming assignment or mission on the planet. You can find details about this in my book "Unlocking Higher Performance—Learning From 24/7 Smart Billionaires & Millionaires™."

Table of Hebraic Meaning of Words & Names Discussed

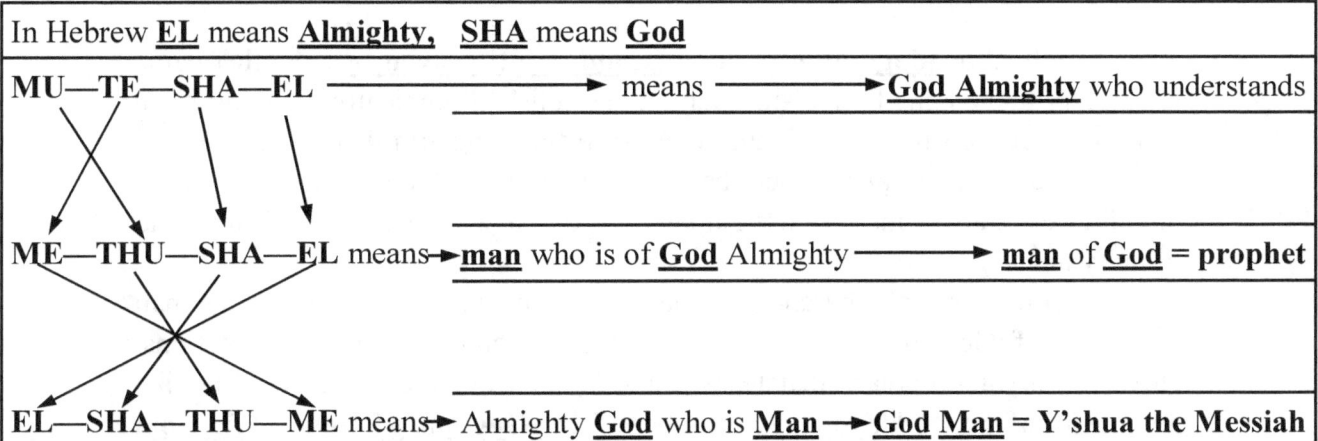

Please reference the above **Table of Hebraic Meaning of Words & Names Discussed**. Me-thu-sha(el) means "**man** who is **of God** Almighty" in the Hebrew language (See Genesis 4:18 (NKJV) in the Bible) (See also page 445 of the Hebrew/Aramaic Dictionary of "The New Strong's Complete Dictionary of Bible Words"—Copyright © 1996 by Thomas Nelson Publishers). When read backwards which becomes El-sha-thu-me, it means "Almighty **God** Who is of **Man**" or "Almighty God with man" or "Immanuel" or "God with us" or "Y'shua the Messiah." Y'shua the Messiah is referred to as God-Man in the Bible.

From my name, Muteshael, you derive the name of a prophet (**man of God**) and the Messiah (**God—Man**) of the world.

The name Me-thu-sha(el), not only did it predict the coming of the Messiah (El-sha-thu-me), but also predicts the coming of God Almighty through my name Muteshael. I am not saying that I am God Almighty, but that my name

Muteshael is symbolic of the coming of the **Kingdom of God** or **Kingdom of Heaven** as Y'shua the Messiah said in various passages and I quote:

> "...and as you go, preach, saying the **Kingdom of Heaven** is at hand." Matthew 10:7 (NKJV).

> "Now after John was put in prison, Jesus came to Galilee, preaching the **gospel** of the **kingdom of God**, and saying, "The time is fulfilled, and the **kingdom of God** is at hand. Repent, and believe in the gospel."" Mark 1:14-15 (NKJV).

> "Now when it was day, He departed and went into a deserted place. And the crowd sought Him and came to Him, and tried to keep Him from leaving them; but He said to them, "I must preach the **kingdom of God** to the other cities also, because for this purpose I have been sent."" Luke 4:42-43 (NKJV).

Calling the **kingdom of God** or **Kingdom of Heaven** by any other name is contrary to the Kingdom Y'shua came to establish. Technically speaking if we were to strictly go by what Y'shua referred to the Kingdom then, when we call ourselves any other labels used based on founders of churches or spiritual beliefs, we are all wrong. We use names to be divisive against Y'shua's teaching of unity in love.

In one sense, all churches, on the planet, which have any other name than Kingdom of God/Heaven are wrong based on above scripture quotations. However, if you do preach that Jesus Christ is Son of God and the only Messiah and Savior of the world, you are a member of the **Kingdom of God** or **Kingdom of Heaven** which must be the only label of us who believe in Y'shua as Savior and Messiah of the world and it doesn't matter the label you wear. The question is, are you a member of a church or religion founded by a man (prophet or not) or a member of the **kingdom of God** or **Kingdom of Heaven** as instituted by Y'shua? Infinitely more important, are we doing what Christ said we must do as we call ourselves Christians?

When Y'shua, after crucifixion said, "It is finished," He meant that all that was needed to establish the Kingdom of God was completed until His second coming, and through His disciples laying hands on those that believed through them the anointing was passed on from those to others that have believed till today. Doctrines of men have been added to the ones commanded by Y'shua, hence the various denominations since the first century. Any important event such as God deciding to take the gospel of His Kingdom off the face of the earth would have been foretold by Y'shua as He foretold all that would happen before His second coming.

I am for uniting in love all who proclaim Y'shua as Son of God and Savior of the world, eschewing divisiveness based on "which is the most correct church" or claims that "our denomination or church is the only true church, others are not." Divisiveness is of the devil and it goes against the teachings of Y'shua in the Bible.

In fact in the Old Testament of the Bible Y'shua is referred to as <u>Mighty God</u> (or El-Sha in Hebrew) in Isaiah 9:4-6 (NKJV) and I quote:

> "For unto us a Child is born, unto us a ***<u>Son</u>*** is given; and the ***<u>government</u>*** will be upon His shoulder. And His name will be called Wonderful, Counselor, ***<u>Mighty God</u>***, Everlasting Father, Prince of ***<u>Peace</u>***. Of the increase of His ***<u>government</u>*** and ***<u>peace</u>*** there will be no end,"

The reason the Christ is referred to as God-Man is because He was ***<u>Mighty God</u>*** in the flesh—in hu***<u>man</u>*** form. Hence His reference to what He was establishing as the **<u>Kingdom of God.</u>** Notice also the fact that the above verse implies that the Christ is in charge of ***<u>government</u>*** on the earth. He is not president or prime minister physically, but He is in control of all ***<u>governments</u>***, hence the importance of nations electing leaders that are Godly in conduct in public and their private lives. Conduct of our leaders both in public and private can affect citizens of a nation.

My last name Mutesha is Hebrew. I changed my name from Mutesha to Mu-te-sha(el) based on the above name in Genesis 4:18 (NKJV). Mu-te-sha(el) means "God Almighty who understands." My name Mu-te-sha(el) reminds me of God Almighty (Sha-el in Hebrew) and Y'shua the Messiah 24/7. Based on my name I refer to myself as a Hebrew of all Hebrews.

More than 2000 years ago (or 28 Generations from the time of Y'shua), when Y'shua the Messiah (known as Jesus Christ) commenced His earthly assignment, He started with only 12 people without Facebook, Twitter, U-Tube or other social networks on the Internet. With only 12 people without modern day technology Y'shua has changed the lives of an untold numbers of people on the planet because Y'shua demonstrated unconditional love to all humanity in deed and word. He loved all regardless of their background. He came for those who were sick—sinners. If you don't show unconditional love to all sinners, **<u>which we all are</u>** (he without sin cast the first stone), and condemn homosexuals and lesbians alone, you can't be of Christ.

Our leaders, spiritual and political on the other hand have failed because they are not driven by the **<u>unconditional love</u>** for humanity, but **<u>power</u>** and the **<u>almighty dollar</u>**, and worst of all, **<u>hate mongering</u>**.

You ordinary Americans, imagine what we can accomplish with over 311,000,000 people for the good of all humanity on the planet! If each of us, the more than 311,000,000 who live in the United States decided to allow unconditional love for all humanity to motivate us so we can mitigate the suffering of all humanity on the planet by helping people help themselves in the USA and surround the globe, we are going to be the greatest generation that ever lived on the planet—the 4th Generation USA. Folks let's do it! Or are we going to be remembered as the generation that allowed the USA to sink deeper into its morass of confusion, divisiveness, deception and depravity? Which one are we going to be?

When Y'shua started His assignment He read from a passage in Isaiah 61:1-2. What He said is documented in Luke 4:18-19 (NKJV)— He said and I quote:

> "The Spirit of the Lord is upon Me, because He has anointed Me to preach the gospel to the **poor**; He has sent Me to heal the **brokenhearted**, to proclaim **liberty** to the **captives** and recovery of sight to the blind, to set at liberty those who are **oppressed**; to proclaim the acceptable year of the Lord."

If you are not a believer in Him in name only, His assignment is your assignment. His assignment is my assignment foremost and the acceptable year is 2011, not 2012.

He also said, in Mark 12:30-31 (NKJV), quoting from Deuteronomy 6:4-5 (NKJV) and Leviticus 19:18 (NKJV) combined, that

> "The first of all the commandments is: 'Hear, O Israel, the Lord our God, the Lord is one. And you shall **love the Lord your God** with all your heart, with all your soul, with all your mind, and with all your strength.' This is the first commandment. And the second, like it, is this: 'You shall **love your neighbor as yourself.**' There is no other commandment greater than these."

If we are not believers in Him in name only, we must put into practice the above two greatest commandments. Which values are we going to follow?

Friends the reason why we have dysfunction in all essential aspects of life is because a lot of us are hypocrites in this country the USA. And so are many others, in other countries, who claim to be believers in Christ—followers in name only.

Please do not misunderstand me, I am not in any way shape or form claiming to be God Almighty or Messiah by sharing the meaning of my name and my mission with you. And I am quoting scripture to simply share scripture that has impacted my life.

On July 3, 2009, when I was in jail, a passage from Isaiah 46:8-13 was fulfilled in my life in Waukegan, Illinois USA. It reads and I quote:

> "Remember this, and show yourselves men; recall to mind, O you transgressors. Remember the former things of old, for I am **God**, and there is no other; I am **God**, and there is none like Me, **declaring the end from the beginning**, and from ancient times things that **are not yet done**, saying, 'My counsel shall stand, and I will do all My pleasure,' calling a bird of prey from the east, **the man who executes My counsel, from a far country**."

Sha in Hebrew means **God** and I am not saying that because my name has **Sha** in it therefore I am **God**, but that my ultimate mission because of the **Sha** is that of **God**. The other part of the verse I am saying was fulfilled in my life is: "**the man**"—an ordinary man, not God-Man, but an ordinary man, not perfect, but strives after God's excellence, not man's, just like you, who carries out God's counsel. In other words a man who gives it all to advocate, practice and implement God's precepts in all essential areas of life—personal, professional, business, political, judicial, social, financial, economical, foreign policy, etc. The other aspect of this verse is that I was born in **a far country**—Zambia, Africa. It is not a coincidence that I was born in Zambia and I am here in the USA executing God's counsel within the US and around the world.

It goes on to say,

> "Indeed I have **spoken** it; I will also **bring it to pass**. I have **purposed it**; I will also **do it**. "Listen to Me, you stubborn-hearted, who are far from righteousness: I bring My righteousness near, it shall not be far off; My salvation shall not linger…"

Remember the predictions I have made till today 2011— God **spoke through me** and He **brought the predictions to pass** because He **purposed** them. God did it. I did not.

Find out from my book, "Unlocking Higher Performance—Learning From 24/7 Smart Billionaires & Millionaires™" more about why I say that the passage Isaiah 46:8-13 was fulfilled in my life.

Whereas my last name Muteshael gives me my spiritual leadership assignment, the names Ronex John Kennedy give me my public spiritedness leadership assignment, not as in politician—I am not and will never be one. A truth teller within the context of what the word of God teaches cannot be a politician or lawyer in the U.S., but as in what I am doing at:

RJJKM 24-7 SmartG.R.O.U.P.Network™.

John Kennedy reminds me of the late (ex)-president *John* Fitzgerald *Kennedy* who said, and I quote portions of his inaugural address:

> "……The world is very different now. For man holds in his mortal hands the power **to abolish all forms of human poverty** and all forms of human life. And yet the same revolutionary beliefs for which our forebears fought are still at issue around the globe—the belief that **the rights of man** come not from the generosity of the state, but from the hand of **God**."

About **global poverty**, JFK goes on to say, and I quote,

> "……To those peoples in the huts and villages **across the globe** struggling to break the bonds of **mass misery**, we **pledge** our best efforts to **help them help themselves**, for whatever period is required—not because the Communists may be doing it, not because we seek their votes, but because **it is right**. If a free society cannot help the many who are poor, it **cannot save the few who are rich**."

His vision still lives in me. Other nations clearly know the intent of our policies of protecting American interests and there is nothing wrong with that. However, when our interests become imperialistic and exploitative, much like the British empire's, let's make no mistake, other nations know it too well. We may succeed in the short-run, but in the long-term, inevitably, failure awaits. Britain is our example. The Soviet Union is another.

What kind of people would be content to be billionaires and millionaires and laugh at the plight of other human beings within the US and outside. Perhaps we are beginning to understand what it feels like to be a beggar at the National level—begging China, a communist nation, to come and rescue us. If the U.S. is where it is today, make no mistake if you are in the top 1% to think that you are invincible—you are not.

Helping others help themselves within and outside the United States is a God-given mission to all of us, regardless of your profession at the individual, national and global level. It is in the process of helping others that we ourselves get helped—greed has a limit and is not sustainable. Helping others is perpetual and is sustained by God Himself.

Ron(ex) reminds me of (ex) president Ron(ald) Wilson Reagan (RWR) who said, and I quote:

> "The time has come for a **new American emancipation**—a great national drive to tear down **economic barriers** and liberate the spirit of **enterprise** in the most **distressed areas** of our country. My friends, together we can do this, and do it we must, so **help me God**. From **new freedom** will spring new opportunities for **growth**, a more **productive**, **fulfilled** and **united people**, and a **stronger America**—an America that will lead the technological revolution, and also open its mind and heart and soul to the treasures of literature, music, and poetry, and the values of faith, courage, and love."

His vision still lives in me. RWR has been out of office for more than 20 years and where we are today tells us what kind of leadership we have had since 1988. RWR advocated economic emancipation for all, hence his partial success.

When education and financial resources are available to all without prejudice, that is how you tear down **economic barriers** and liberate the spirit of **enterprise** in the most **distressed areas** within and outside the US. When that happens we are going to have a bigger percentage of Americans who are financially independent creating **growth** and enhancing **productivity**. When the 99% is as **fulfilled** as the top 1%, America will be **united** and **stronger**.

It is therefore in the interest of the top 1% to help the 99%, not for the sake of the 99%, but the top 1% and their own salvation as JFK wisely stated, "If a free society cannot help the many who are poor, it **cannot save the few who are rich**.".

If our founding fathers were not deceptive and divisive in the framing of the declaration of independence and drafting of the U.S. Constitution, slavery would have been abolished in 1787, the U.S. Constitution would not have been amended 27 times and 625,000 lives that perished during the Civil War would have been saved. All minorities including Caucasian women wouldn't have had to fight for their rights. By design the USA was built to cater to a few people, the elite of society, not all Americans as the Occupy Wall Street has so revealed.

The whole nation and the planet for that matter has come to this awakening because everybody is affected. Minorities, especially African Americans knew the system was dysfunctional right from the beginning based on their experiences. If it had to take the 99% to be slaves to the top 1% to realize that the system was dysfunctional, it goes to show how depraved human beings can be—our failure to feel for other human beings and I am as guilty as the founding fathers were and as the top 1% is today.

When I managed to start my small expedited delivery business I became judgmental as to why others were not making it—especially Black people like me. It wasn't until I was falsely accused and imprisoned and listened to more than a hundred stories of all Americans and non-Americans of all races that I understood their plight. Yes, sometimes it takes experience to empathize, but folks, some issues are basic: Has anyone in their right mind ever volunteered to be a slave or to be treated differently in a dishonorable manner?

What's hard about understanding that we all must pay the same percentage in taxes and that not everyone in society will ever be rich at the same time?

I wholeheartedly support the Occupy Wall Street movement, the Tea Partiers, ordinary Democrats and Republicans who are sick and tired of being sick and tired and I am saying let's unite in this militancy I am calling the RJJKM'S Global Revolution.

That is why we can't forget civil rights activists of all minorities who saw the iniquities in the system and did something about it.

Not to minimize the impact of other civil rights leaders of minorities, I believe Dr. Martin Luther King Jr., who epitomizes peaceful civil disobedience for the right cause, is a great example in light of the times then in the sixties. His message is as true today as it was then, and today we fight for all races. From his I have a dream speech, which is still appropriate today, I quote portions of it as a reminder to all of us—it's about joining hands because America and the planet can't afford blood-shed:

> "I have a dream that my four little children will one day live in a nation where they will not be judged by the color of their skin but by the content of their character……And when this happens, when we allow freedom to ring, when we let it ring from every village and every hamlet, from every state and every city, we will be able to speed up that day when all of God's children, Black men and White men, Jews and Gentiles, Protestants and Catholics, will be able to join hands and sing in the words of the old Negro spiritual, "Free at last! free at last! thank God Almighty, we are free at last!"

His vision still lives in me. Unity across race, color and religious beliefs—eschewing divisiveness and deception in our policies as a nation and global community. A house that is divided cannot stand and that applies to nations too.

I can't forget other great leaders on the planet—Kenneth Kaunda (during the struggle for independence in Zambia), Mahatma Ghandhi (India), Nelson Mandela (South Africa), Abraham Lincoln (USA), and many others I have not mentioned in the USA and other nations.

The U.S. Constitution as is, even if I were born in the United States I would never consider running for the president of the USA because, as impeccable as my background is, without repealing the entire U.S. Constitution, I would be setting myself up for failure as it has been for all presidents including Mr. Barack Obama.

Even with all indicators, that is, my education, experience, performance and being spiritually in tune with what is going on the planet, and that I so desire to lead the United States into a better place as president, I could not consider it, not because of the clause that says you have to be born here, but that **I could not in all God consciousness defend the U.S. Constitution** as is because that would be endorsing all it was designed to be—an oppressive instrument to Caucasian women, African slaves, Native Americans, other minorities and other Caucasians who were considered inferior to our founding fathers. I told you that I am not a politician—I am a truth teller.

Therefore, if everyone understands what I am talking about, which I believe everyone does, then there is no need wasting time repealing the entire U. S. Constitution. Why continue using a document that has failed all of us within the United States and outside? Continued use of this document means we continue getting the same results in all our systems and projects. To make government work the way it is supposed to work in a **real free enterprise system** the U.S. Constitution needs to be repealed. There is no need for debate—the proof is in the pudding.

Let me emphasize this in a very dramatic fashion—**secularism is a vote for the devil** and the way he goes about doing business in all essential areas of life. **Secularism is a vote against Almighty God** and His enduring principles in His sacred writings of Holy Scriptures. So the choice is really between what is right in the sight of Almighty God or what is right in the sight of the Devil. I choose Almighty God. Who is your choice?

At this point I have to say what Moses said to the children of Israel in Exodus 32:26 (NKJV), and I quote,

"Whoever is on the LORD'S side—come to me!"

Moses was addressing the 4th Generation of Hebrews who were seared in the manacles of slavery and injustice, who after being liberated out of slavery in Egypt, rejected God. The 4th Generation of the USA and the 28th Generation of the planet from the time of Y'shua of all races are in the same predicament today—victims of dysfunctional systems in society world wide today—slaves if you will, to our leaders and the rich and powerful. Victims of choices our founding fathers made.

The 1st generation of the USA rejected God after being liberated from the Tyrannical rule of Great Britain. It is to all that I make the statement—**"Whoever is on the LORD'S side—come to me!"** In our case I am saying, if you believe in Almighty God—the LORD, let's join hands for the sake of humanity within and outside the United States, pray and act so God's kingdom will come and His will be done on earth as it is in heaven.

The proof that any system put in place works, comes out of seeing the results from it, be it, Spiritual, Judicial, Political, Educational, Financial, Economical or Social.

Friends after being a nation for 235 years this year 2011, the following is the net result of the U.S. Constitution and all the laws in the USA. Unfortunately <u>*woes/dysfunctions*</u> in the USA are the same ones facing the entire planet because we have been copied by other nations.

CHAPTER 8

DYSFUNCTIONS/WOES/PROBLEMS FACING THE USA AND THE PLANET

Financial & Economic Issues

- Through the Marshall Plan we, the United States, were able to <u>lend</u> money to war-torn Europe—now we are the borrowers; from China, of all nations, whose leaders are oppressive to its citizens. What happened?
- The U.S. debt is at more than $14 trillion, the budget deficit is at more than $1.3 trillion, debt per tax payer is at more than $129,000, debt per citizen at more than $46,000 according to the real time USDebtClock.org statistics on May 19, 2011 at 8:00 p.m.
- According to the U.S. Census Bureau report of May 19, 2011, "the Nation's international trade deficit in goods and services increased to $48.2 billion in March from $45.4 billion (revised) in February, as imports increased more than exports—a whopping $48.2 billion.
- Unemployment is pandemic—Our political operative Mitt Romney, a multimillionaire, was teasing the unemployed saying he too was unemployed; how insensitive!

According to an article by William S. Lerach, posted on February 26, 2011 11:32 AM on Huffpost Politics website entitled "Blame Wall Street, Not Hard Working Americans, for the Pension Funds Fiasco, he says and I quote portions of it:

- Before today we had the 1929 Market Crash, a wealth destruction event that <u>ended the dreams of an American generation</u>.
- Then came the S&L blowup of the mid-1980s. <u>Over 3,000 S&Ls collapsed</u>.
- A few years later it was the 2000-2001 dot.com/telecommunications meltdowns epitomized by WorldCom and Enron.
- Most recently, our major <u>financial institutions were rocked by scandal</u> -- the worst crash since 1929.
- Investors lost over <u>$20 trillion in these three massive wealth destruction events, which were the result of the teardown of the regulatory framework that had been erected over the prior 70 years to control our financial markets and protect investors.</u>
- America's <u>public pension plans</u> -- guardians of the life savings of countless

working people -- were the biggest victims of these wealth destruction events.
- As a result, the financial situation of our <u>public employee pension funds is precarious</u>. These funds lost <u>hundreds of billions</u> in the S&L disaster and the 2001-2002 market crash.
- Then, in the 2008-2009 financial crisis, the losses of public funds were stupendous. <u>109 state funds lost $865 billion in about one year</u>. CalPERS lost $72 billion! Now virtually all of these funds are now grossly under-funded. New Jersey and Illinois are each over <u>$50 billion</u> underwater.
- <u>Public employee funds are probably $3 or $4 trillion underwater</u>.

Health Issues

—Serious Mental Illness In the USA
- "Serious mental illnesses (SMIs), which afflict about 6% of American adults, cost society <u>$193.2 billion</u> in lost earnings per year," according to findings published by American Journal of Psychiatry......"Each year the economic cost of untreated mental illness is staggering — over <u>$100 billion</u> on untreated mental health disorders and $400 billion on addiction disorders,"..... "Our country cannot afford to continue losing $500 billion a year to these treatable diseases." More than <u>13 million</u> adult Americans are suffering from SMI.

—AIDS/HIV On The Planet
- According to former President Bill Clinton, when he gave his speech at IPA in the Hyatt Regency of Chicago, Saturday, December 8, 2001 he said, "But if just you take AIDS—we have 40 million AIDS cases—25 million people have died of AIDS. 70% of the cases are in Africa, but the fastest growing rates of AIDS are in the former Soviet Union, on Europe's back door. The second fastest growing rates are in the Caribbean on America's front door.....The third fastest growing rates are in India,.....which has about 10 million cases now—more than any country outside Africa. The fourth big rate and problem is in China.....which just admitted they have twice as many cases as they had previously thought, and only 4% of the adults have any idea how AIDS is contracted and spread." According to UNAIDS, there were almost 2 million people living with AIDS at the end of 2001 in the U.S., Latin America, Canada and Caribbean.

Global Poverty

- About world poverty Mr. Clinton said, we should change "....conditions in poor nations to make progress more possible" and he gives reasons why this must be done. Mr. Clinton goes on to say, "Half the people live on less than $2 a day. In the world today, a billion people live on less than $1 a day. A billion people go to bed hungry every night. A billion and a half people never get a clean glass of water, and one woman dies every minute in childbirth—all because of global poverty."

U.S Wars

- Because of the Constitution of the United States more than half a million people died during the Civil War.
- As of June 2011, the U.S. was still involved in three wars.
- It cost $3 trillion to capture Osama bin Laden over 15 years.

The above woes are a tremendous burden on all of us and yet the list above is not exhaustive. **The United States is too important to fail**, not just to Americans, but the planet as a whole. **No nation is unimportant—all nations are important**, hence my call on all of us citizens of the planet to work to together to solve problems we are facing together. In the U.S. both the Republican and Democratic leadership have contributed to the demise of these United States. I know you agree with me. If you agree with me, read my plan of action at my website and my book, "Unlocking Higher Performance: Learning From 24-7 Smart Billionaires and Millionaires."

Dysfunctions (woes) in society including, unfortunately the USA are proof that systems in place right here in the USA and surround the globe are not working. Our leaders in the United States and other countries have failed to provide solutions to the problems we face today, hence my call on all of you who are not professional politicians to rise to the challenge of finding those solutions we so desperately need. Let us be pioneers to a new America and a new planet where all citizens, great and small, of the planet get involved in this global brainstorming effort to make the world a better place.

The US is a nation of peoples from all over the planet and I know that we all care about those left in other places outside the US. All of us, including Native Americans, came from other parts of the planet, we are all aliens when it comes down to it. We care about those outside of the US because of our ancestral ties, and therefore we can't be free if they are not free in every sense of the word freedom.

And so it is within. **The top 1% cannot be free if the 99% are not free**, and this freedom of all humanity within and without can only come through a

*F*reedom *I*ndeed *RE*volution—***F.I.RE***—the unconditional love of all humanity. The acronym ***F.I.RE*** is appropriate, in that, to get fine GOLD it needs to go through the fire. So it is with all of us, unless we go through difficulty times we can't be refined in our intent toward others. The refining of our human spirit doesn't come about through acquiring billions of dollars and material wealth, the Father of all spirits, Yahweh, is the refiner of all because He knows what it will take for all of us to change as individuals and nations.

Therefore, if the "change we can believe in" is a human being, we get disappointed and we have, haven't we? If we put "country first" and not God, we get disappointed because the US is broke and yet we had put our trust in it. Our Savior China is having its own problems. The Asian tiger, Japan, apparently can't control natural disasters with all its smart technologies and neither have we, the United States. The Soviet Union is no more. REALITY CHECK! Which leaves us with one option—GOD. That's why we can't secure the United States outside of the global context without God's aid.

For the Continental forces, under the leadership of George Washington to defeat well organized forces of the British empire, we all agree, God was involved. However, did God get involved so we can turn around and become tyrannical to those under our leadership? Absolutely not. God intervened in the slavery issue and unfortunately through bloodshed.

Our leadership should not make another grave and deadly mistake of saying the militancy that has engulfed the US and the world around will go away. No it will not. Why do I believe that? Read the Bible—Almighty God abhors greed, oppression, involuntary servitude and other evil deportments. It is God Himself speaking through all—Occupy Wall Street, Tea Partiers, the fed-up Democrats and Republicans and everyone else.

Leaders, heed the voice of the people within and outside the United States.

CHAPTER 9

—RE-FOUNDING THE UNITED STATES—
WHAT ARE THE ROOT CAUSES OF DYSFUNCTIONS/WOES/ PROBLEMS? WHAT ARE THE SOLUTIONS?

Solutions: First thing First—the U.S. Constitution

Ivy league education has failed us in the USA because it has produced liberals, conservatives and moderates all of whom are basically in Washington D.C. to stand in the way of real progress:

A conservative is a person, man or woman, who has a perfect brain, which he/she conserves—doesn't use it, and accomplishes nothing.

A liberal is a person, man or woman, who has a perfect brain, which he/she uses liberally—aimlessly—no profound goals, and accomplishes nothing.

A moderate is a person, man or woman, who has a perfect brain, but can't decide what to be—liberal or conservative. When a moderate looks at both conservatives and liberals he/she sees that nothing significant is being done by both conservatives and liberals as a result he/she becomes confused—which results in a moderate accomplishing nothing.

The question is: what are politicians and lawyers good for? Lying!!!

What do you get when you cross a politician and a lawyer? A liar squared!!!

I call them lying squirrels (liar squared)—good for "nothing." I meant to say good for "nuts." Get it? Squirrels are head over hills with "nuts." Politicians and lawyers are head over hills with accomplishing "nothing" for citizens of the planet.

That is where it's at today in the world. Are you surprised?

The U.S. Constitution was deliberately and through oversight designed to promote the above dysfunction of accomplishing nothing.

Please read my book and start doing something wherever you are NOW!!! The above issues are the essence and the reasons why I decided to get involved.

This is not a political or religious crusade movement, it is simply a movement about helping people help themselves in the USA and every human being on the planet—Africa, North and South America, Asia, Middle East, Europe, New Zealand, Australia, every nation on the planet.

All our leaders seem to invoke the name of God in their injunctions and addresses to the nation, but our Constitution rejects our reliance upon God—in other words we have paid lip-service to God. Our Constitution is supreme to God's sacred scriptures. Should we be surprised at the dysfunctions in our society because we have dishonored the Almighty? In order for us to experience ultimate spiritual blessings and material prosperity we must now bring back God in the public arena by re-founding the USA to secure a better future for all our kids.

My story of 27 years in the United States has been one of being literally re-enslaved, exploited and oppressed among other things. America is still practicing slavery. Prisons and mental institutions are not a form of slavery for Blacks, it is clandestine slavery even with Barack as president and Oprah Winfrey as a billionaire in the United States.

To understand my mission completely today, I had to go through everything I have been through, like the Lord Y'shua—I see God's hand written all over it. Like the prophet Jeremiah writes and I quote:

> "Then the word of the LORD came to me, saying: "Before I formed you in the womb I knew you; before you were born I **sanctified** you; I **ordained** you a prophet to the nations." Jeremiah 1:4-5 (NKJV).

It is not a coincidence, today, that Barack is in the office of the president in the United States. I was born, sanctified and ordained for such a time as this. I want you to join me so we can complete what Abraham Lincoln started, what JFK, Malcom X, Martin Luther King Jr., Ronald Wilson Reagan, etc. have propelled forward. It is time for completion in the 4th Generation of the United States and the 28th generation on the planet from the time of Christ.

On **Good Friday**, we celebrate the death of our Lord Y'SHUA the CHRIST who died on the cross to redeem mankind from eternal death—condemned by his sinfulness. Within the meaning of my last name lies my ultimate purpose in this life. Muteshael which means "Almighty God who understands" in Hebrew derived African languages, Lamba and Kaonde, my ultimate mission on the planet is to do what is right in the sight of the Almighty. I extrapolate the meaning of my last name further by saying that, it is only Almighty God who understands the plight of his creation on the planet that can lead us out of the global woes we face today.

When **Methushael** appears on the scene to the **4th** Generation of his time (**4th** Descendant of Cain), people begin to worship **GOD** again. Why did they stop? They stopped because they were stunned and shocked at the killing of ABEL by his brother CAIN. This was the first death of a human being. Methushael leads his **4th** Generation into **GOD'S** spiritual blessing and prosperity.

Though CAIN was a murderer, God allowed him to be productive. He built a city he named after his son Enoch in the land of Nod. Contrary to popular misconception CAIN was not a wanderer on the planet. If he was, he wouldn't have built a city, which is a huge undertaking. Much like Cain so are our founding fathers who were responsible for 625,000 people who were murdered over the issue of slavery. May we never forget because history is repeating itself—the top 1% versus the 99%.

On page 445 of the Hebrew/Aramaic Dictionary of "The New Strong's Complete Dictionary of Bible Words", Methushael is referred to as an antediluvian patriarch (rōshē abōth in Hebrew) which means he existed before Noah's flood and was a **_founder_** of one of the ancient Hebrew families (See also Webster's New World Dictionary of the American Language, Second College Edition).

My lineage as a Hebrew, through my name, **Muteshael**, can be traced all the way to Genesis through the name **Methushael**. Whereas **Methushael** was a **_founder_**, **Muteshael** is a **_re-founder_**.

In Genesis 17:1-7 (NKJV) it says about Abraham who was a Hebrew and I quote:

> When Abram was ninety-nine years old, the Lord appeared to Abram and said to him, "I am **_Almighty God (El Sha)_**; walk before Me and be **_blameless_**. And I will make My **_covenant_** between Me and you, and will **_multiply you exceedingly_**." Then Abram fell on his face, and God talked with him, saying: "As for Me, behold, My **_covenant is with you_**, and you shall be a **_father of many nations_**. No longer shall your name be called Abram, but your name shall be Abraham; for I have made you a father of many nations. I will make you exceedingly fruitful; and I will make **_nations of you_**, and **_kings shall come from you_**. And I will establish My **_covenant between Me and you_** and your **_descendants after you in their generations_**, for an **_everlasting covenant_**, to be God **(Sha)** to you and your descendants after you.

Pay special attention to the **_underlined bold italicized_** text, especially, "**_kings shall come from you_**" phrase. Not only were kings promised in the lineage of Abraham, a Hebrew, it was through Isaac that the promised messiah Y'shua (El-Sha-thu-me) would arise. Did Sha_El (God Almighty in English) cease raising His leaders with the death of Christ on the cross? On the contrary! The Almighty said and I quote:

> "And I will establish My **_covenant between Me and you_** and

your *descendants after you in their generations*, for an *everlasting covenant*, to be God to you and your descendants after you."

28 Generations ago Y'shua, who was God in the flesh, a descendant of Abraham, Isaac, Jacob and King David, through His earthly mother Mary established a New Covenant with all humanity—not just with us Hebrews, but all nations, languages and ethnicities on the planet.

Timeline From Genesis to 2008 Of Prominent Leadership
—Methushael to Muteshael—

- From the time of Methushael, **4th** descendant of Cain (**His name reversed prophesied of the Messiah**) to Abraham it is about **21 generations.**

- From the time of Methushael to Moses (who appeared to the **4th Generation** of the Hebrews in Egypt) it is approximately **28 generations.**

- From the time of Abraham to David it is **14 generations.**

- From the time of David (**who prophesied of the Messiah**) into Captivity it is 14 generations.

- From the time of Captivity to **JESUS CHRIST** (El-sha-thu-me) it is 14 generations.

- From the time of **David** to **JESUS CHRIST** it is **28 generations.**

- From the time of **JESUS CHRIST** to RJJK **Muteshael** (who appears to the **4th Generation** of the USA) (2008) it is about **28 generations** of the planet.

If you use 70 or 72 years as the average life span of human beings on the planet, and you divide 2008 by 71 you get **28.2** generations give or take. You can't be more precise than that.

This time around, I believe and know that, I **Muteshael,** like **Methushael** was to his **4th** generation, as **David** was to his **14th** generation from Abraham, as **Moses** was to the **4th** generation of the Hebrews in Egypt, **28** generations from Methushael, and as our Lord **JESUS CHRIST** was to the **1st** Century generation or **28th** generation from King **David,** I am addressing **4th** Generation USA and the **28th** Generation of the planet from the time of **JESUS CHRIST**!! This is my assignment in God's infinite scheme of things.

The Almighty God has consistently raised prominent kings, prophets and ultimately the Messiah in **generational** times specified above and as covenanted with Abraham to this day.

The United States is in it's 4th Generation. If you use 75 years as the average life span of an American and you divide 235 by 75 you get 3.13 generations. We are 10 years into the 4th USA Generation.

Time Line of USA Presidents Pertinent to My Calling
—George Washington To *Ron*ex *John Kennedy* Muteshael—

George Washington, 1st USA President
1st Generation USA

John Fitzgerald *Kennedy*, 35th USA President
3rd Generation USA

Ron(ald) Wilson Reagan, **40th** USA President
3rd Generation USA

Ron(ex) James *John Kennedy* Muteshael **45th** USA President
4th Generation USA

Do you see a pattern? God's pattern!! I had nothing to do with it. What are the chances that the Almighty is not involved in what happens at the individual, national and global level? Friend He is. You can chose to "ostracize" Him which you can't or reject Him which you can—when it comes down to it He is sovereign and all of us are subject to Him, mighty or not.

God Is Indeed Involved In The Affairs Of Human Beings
—Proof Positive—

What are the chances that God was not involved and will not be involved in my life? None. He was and will be involved in my life:

- What are the chances that God is involved in our affairs that Methushael would show up as a patriarch (**founder**) to his **4th** generation and I Muteshael would show up to 4th generation USA as a **re-founder? Highly likely to infinity!**
- What are the chances that God is involved in our affairs that from the time of Methushael to Moses (who appeared to the **4th Generation** of the Hebrews in Egypt) it is **28 generations** and it is **28 generations** from the time of Christ to today and I **Muteshael would show up to 4th Generation** USA?

Highly likely to infinity!
- What are the chances that God is involved in our affairs that from the time of **David** to **JESUS CHRIST** it is **28 generations** and from the time of **JESUS CHRIST** to **Ron**(ex) James **John Kennedy Muteshael** (who appears to the **4th** Generation of the USA) (2008) it is about **28 generations** of the planet? **Highly likely to infinity!**

In Genesis 15:15-16 (NKJV) it says and I quote,

"Now when the sun was going down, a deep sleep fell upon Abram; and behold, horror *and* great darkness fell upon him. Then He said to Abram: "Know certainly that your descendants will be strangers in a land *that is* not theirs, and will serve them, and they will afflict them *four hundred years*. And also the nation whom they serve *I will judge*; afterward they shall come out with great possessions. Now as for you, you shall go to your fathers in peace; you shall be buried at a good old age. But in the *fourth generation* they shall return here, for the *iniquity of the Amorites* is *not yet complete*."

In churches in the US we talk about slavery in Egypt intensely and dramatize rescue of my Hebrew brothers and sisters by God and gloss over slavery and oppression of all peoples of all races really in the United States and yet the tragedy here in the US is worse by all accounts including loss of human life. Has it changed?

It is 4th Generation in the U.S. today and the U.S. is experiencing God's *judgment* the same way Egypt did. We lost 625,000 people over slavery. How many people died in Egypt compared to the US during the Civil War? My guess is that it was much less than 625,000. The truth. Which path are we going to take—denial and pretend that our leaders of either party are going to save us? Or face up to the truth. Facts and dysfunctions are glaring at us. It is the 99% that are paying the price of mediocre, visionless and spineless leadership of both the Democratic and Republican parties.

We are borrowing

"Now it shall come to pass, if you diligently obey the voice of the Lord your God, to observe carefully all His commandments which I command you today, that the Lord your God will set you **high above all nations of the earth**. And all these blessings shall come upon you and overtake you, **because you obey the voice of the Lord your God**: "Blessed *shall* you *be* in the city, and blessed *shall* you *be* in the country. "Blessed *shall be* the fruit of your body, the produce of your ground and the increase of your herds, the increase of your cattle and the offspring of your flocks. "Blessed *shall be* your basket and your kneading bowl. "Blessed *shall* you *be* when you come in, and blessed *shall* you *be* when you go out. "The Lord will cause your enemies who rise against you to be defeated before your face; they shall come out against you one way and flee before you seven ways"........"The Lord will establish you as a holy people to Himself, just as He has sworn to you, if you keep the commandments of the Lord your God and walk in His ways....... **"You shall lend to many nations, but you shall not borrow."** *Deuteronomy 28:—(NKJV)*

We Lent Money To War-Torn Europe (many nations), by the Grace of God
"The **Marshall Plan** (officially the **European Recovery Program, ERP**) was the large-scale American program to aid Europe where the United States gave monetary support to help rebuild European economies after the end of World War II in order to combat the spread of Soviet communism. The plan was in operation for four years beginning in April 1948. The goals of the United States were to rebuild a war-devastated region, remove trade barriers, modernize industry, and make Europe prosperous again. The initiative was named after Secretary of State George Marshall. The plan had bipartisan support in Washington, where the Republicans controlled Congress and the Democrats controlled the White House. The Plan was largely the creation of State Department officials, especially William L. Clayton and George F. Kennan. Marshall spoke of urgent need to help the European recovery in his address at Harvard University in June 1947. The reconstruction plan, developed at a meeting of the participating European states, was established on June 5, 1947. It offered the same aid to the Soviet Union and its allies, but they did not accept it. During the four years that the plan was operational, US $13 billion in economic and technical assistance was given to help the recovery of the European countries that had joined in the Organization for European Economic Co-operation. This $13 billion was in the context of a U.S. GDP of $258 billion in 1948, and was on top of $12 billion in American aid to Europe between the end of the war and the start of the Plan that is counted separately from the Marshall Plan. The Marshall Plan

was replaced by the Mutual Security Plan at the end of 1951."
From Wikipedia, the free encyclopedia.

CHINA SAYS TO THE USA, "THE GOOD OLD DAYS OF BORROWING ARE OVER."

Have we kept the commandments of the Lord our God and walked in His ways? NO!

Many people in the United States do not understand that the root causes of all woes we face in the United States and on the planet are directly linked to the answer NO above whether we choose to believe it or not.

In Exodus 34:6-7 (NKJV), it says and I quote,

"Now the Lord descended in the cloud and stood with him there, and proclaimed the name of the Lord. And the Lord passed before him and proclaimed, "The Lord, the Lord God, merciful and gracious, longsuffering, and abounding in goodness and truth, keeping mercy for thousands, forgiving iniquity and transgression and sin, ***by no means clearing the guilty, visiting the iniquity of the fathers*** upon the children and the children's children to the ***third and the fourth generation.***"

The dysfunctions and woes we face today are self-inflicted through the actions of our leaders in our country these United States for obstinately standing in the way of doing what is right in the sight of the Almighty for all Americans. Do we have all the time to do something before we experience worse disasters fashioned by the Almighty Himself? I say the time to act is now.

The United States has been used to prove that the Bible is indeed true. That Almighty God is LORD, Yahweh of the Universe and that both the heavens and the earth (all nations mighty or not) are subject to Him. And therefore because the USA has violated God's spiritual laws since 1776, we are suffering consequences associated with those violations—the 3rd and 4th Generations as stated in the above passage.

Now that we know that God is real, no matter how we feel and that He is the greatest equalizer there ever was and that He is intervening in the plight of the 99%, our leadership must heed the voice of the 99%.

We need to re-found the USA to eliminate dysfunction so we can change the course of our nation for our children's future's sake by implementing my Seven 24/7 Smart System of Core Values.

Therefore my new Global Revolution to me has come to mean, bringing to bear the prophetic visions of God Almighty and the Lord Y'shua the Christ by the power of the Holy Spirit and saying, it is only by understanding that God Almighty is involved in our lives, and that, until all people (men and women; Black, Brown, Red, Yellow and White) are spiritually free indeed from the grip of the evil one and in turn pursue morally upright lives, abandoning sexual depravity, nurture family, render Godly justice, promote real democratic political, economic, and financial freedom for all people on Planet Earth, we cannot be free.

To that end, my 7 fold ultimate goal, must be directed as follows through a 24/7 Smart System of Core Values:

My Seven 24/7 Smart System of Core Values

1. Above all else to promote a spiritual freedom system—a free indeed mentality; love of God and love of your neighbor as yourself. The Golden Rule of life.
2. Promote a moral uprightness system at all levels of community from top to bottom, an integrated and united society across the nation and surround the globe, and family love and unity.
3. Promote a real political freedom system, free of racism, prejudice and divisiveness, real free enterprise and not exploitative capitalism nor oppressive communism or socialism or other isms out there.
4. Promote a universal-the-best-available educational, intellectual development, professional development and health care system as a mandate and a right to all humanity to eliminate illiteracy and preservation of health without regard to income. All human life deserves it and is worth the cost. Government must ensure employees are paid based on education, experience and most importantly performance.
5. (1) Promote an economic, financial and infrastructure system that is based on real free enterprise perpetuating job creation by liberating the spirit of enterprise in all people, through technological creativity and innovation, free of corruption and greed facilitated by the federal government with minimum government intervention. (2) The presidency must be a performance based position and nobody should be guaranteed 4 years if their performance is poor in 1000 days or 3 years from getting into the position. (3) A balanced budget must be a requirement every year. (4) Small and medium sized business development must be given top priority as they are the back bone of the economy. (5) To ensure more successful businesses in the economy, professional business advice must be given to every start-

up operation without fail. (6) Full capitalization must be ensured to promote success. (7) A minimum tax rate that doesn't tax Americans into servitude or put businesses out must be established, and only ordinary Americans who are mostly affected by it must vote to effect change of rate, not the Congress and/or the Senate.

6. Promote a real justice for all system which doesn't favor neither the rich and powerful nor the poor by eliminating loop holes that tend to favor any group of people and denies justice to others.
7. Promote a foreign policy that seeks to build peaceful coalitions, both socially and trade-wise with all peace loving nations on earth, abandoning coercion and divisiveness based on regions of the world; all nations helping one another help each other since all nations on earth are interdependent and God Almighty rules the earth.

Details of these core values are in my book "RJJKM'S Global Revolution—Awakening the USA to its authentic global leadership role."

CHAPTER 10

CONSEQUENCES OF DEVIATING FROM REAL FREE ENTERPRISE

The reality is that no man or nation can undo the path on which we are headed as citizens of the planet, not even I in my own strength and wisdom—only God can and will if we do what is right in His sight—**REAL FREE ENTERPRISE**-not exploitative capitalism—underpaying workers into servitude and the rich refusing to pay an equal percentage in taxes.

In Jeremiah 18:7-10 (NKJV) the LORD says:

> "The instant I speak concerning a nation and concerning a kingdom, **_to pluck up, to pull down, and to destroy it_**, if that nation against whom I have spoken **_turns from its evil_**, I **_will relent of the disaster that I thought to bring upon it_**. And the instant I speak concerning a nation and concerning a kingdom, **_to build and to plant it_**, if it does evil in My sight so that it **_does not obey My voice_**, then I will **_relent concerning the good with which I said I would benefit it_**.
>
> "Now therefore, speak to the men of Judah and to the inhabitants of Jerusalem, saying, 'Thus says the Lord: **_"Behold, I am fashioning a disaster and devising a plan against you. Return now every one from his evil way, and make your ways and your doings good_**.""'"

Has the US been exempted from God's judgment even though God aided its becoming a nation? No. Unless you want to spin the truth. I know its tough to swallow the truth because we are the United States—the greatest nation on the planet contributing 25% to the world GDP. The British empire extended over 25% of the earth and the British boasted saying that "The sun never sets in the British empire." What happened to the empire? Are we a duplicate of that empire? If we are, signs are that we are headed in the same direction.

If all presidents through president #16 had read Jeremiah 34:12-22 (NKJV), we would have averted the Civil War. I must bring this up because all signs are pointing to a Civil War between the haves (top 1%) and have-nots (99%).

The founding fathers had no intention of abolishing slavery

How do we reconcile the declaration of independence in 1776 with the continued existence of slavery till today in a Christian Nation?

While **Thomas Jefferson** crafted the declaration of independence as a leading member of the second continental congress, he also actively participated in ensuring Religious Freedom while Black people were enslaved and White women were considered property.

James Madison is referred to as the "Father of the Constitution," which means he endorsed slavery wholeheartedly.

James Monroe's solution to freedom for Black people was to send them back to Africa, which resulted in the founding of Liberia and other locales for people from the Diaspora.

Of the first 6 presidents **John Quincy Adams** became a leading anti-slavery advocate.

Andrew Jackson signed the Indian Removal Act, which resulted in tens of thousands of Native Americans dying from exposure, hunger, and disease. **Jackson** also banned mailing anti-slavery literature. What a cruel policy!

Millard Fillmore president # 13 said, **"God knows that I detest slavery, but it is an existing evil, for which we are not responsible, and we must endure it….till we can get rid of it without destroying the last hope of free government in the world."**

God knows? Who was he fooling for him to even mention the name of **God** in the same sentence where he advocates preservation of **slavery** in favor **of free government?** Can a people have a free government where slavery and racism exist?

President # 14 **Franklin Pierce**, said, **"I believe that involuntary servitude, as it exists in different States of this Confederacy, is recognized by the Constitution. I believe that it stands like any other admitted right, and that the States where it exists are entitled to efficient remedies to enforce the constitution provisions."**

President # 15, **James Buchanan**, said about the slavery debate that it was **"a matter of but little practical importance."** And immediately after he takes office the Supreme Court ruled in Dred Scott v. Sandford that, **"the federal government had no constitutional right to ban slavery from the territories."** The Supreme Court!!!!

That sentiment still exists in the hearts of some judges, like Judge Stride, Judge Collins, Judge Philips, Judge Fink, and many others with whom I have so far interacted in modern day America though the laws have outlawed **involuntary servitude**.

America was created to be a role model in righteousness as partakers of God's covenant with the patriarch Abraham through Jesus Christ—to be a blessing to others within and outside the US.

America, using its Constitution, the drafting of which was presided over by George Washington, who was a slave owner, deliberately chose for America, to be a land of slavery. George Washington—a Christian! Which Bible did he read?

The bad news is that our Country is still the biggest slave plantation. This time around 99% of Americans (Black, Brown, Red, Yellow and White) are really slaves while the top 1% that own 40% of wealth in America amass billions into their greedy coffers.

Nothing much has changed compared to before 1776. Howard Zinn, in the "People's History of the United States," writes and I quote,

> "Spain was recently unified, one of the new modern nation-states, like France, England, and Portugal. Its population, mostly poor peasants, worked for the nobility, who were ***2 percent of the population and owned 95 percent of the land***. Spain had tied itself to the Catholic Church, expelled all the Jews, driven out the Moors. Like other states of the modern world, Spain sought ***gold***, which was becoming the new mark of wealth, more useful than land because it could buy anything….Spain decided to gamble on a long sail across an unknown ocean. In return for bringing back gold and spices, they promised Columbus ***10 percent of the profits, governorship over new-found lands, and the fame that would go with a new title: Admiral of the Ocean Sea.*** He was a merchant's clerk from the Italian city of Genoa, part-time weaver (the son of a skilled weaver), and expert sailor. He set out with three sailing ships, the largest of which was the *Santa Maria*, perhaps 100 feet long, and thirty-nine crew members."

At the beginning of the first chapter Howard Zinn, in the "People's History of the United States," writes and I quote,

> "Arawak men and women, naked, tawny, and full of wonder, emerged from their villages onto the island's beaches and swam out to get a closer look at the strange big boat. When Columbus and his sailors came ashore, carrying swords, speaking oddly, the Arawaks ran to greet them, ***brought them food, water, gifts***. He later wrote of this in his log: They . . . brought us parrots and balls of cotton and spears and many other things, which they exchanged for the glass beads and hawks' bells. ***They willingly traded everything they owned***. . . . They were well-built, with

good bodies and handsome features. . . . They do not bear arms, and do not know them, for I showed them a sword, they took it by the edge and cut themselves out of ignorance. They have no iron. Their spears are made of cane. . . . ***They would make fine servants. . . . With fifty men we could subjugate them all and make them do whatever we want***. These Arawaks of the Bahama Islands were much like Indians on the mainland, who were ***remarkable (European observers were to say again and again) for their hospitality, their belief in sharing***. These traits did not stand out in the Europe of the Renaissance, dominated as it was by the ***religion of popes***, the ***government of kings***, the ***frenzy for money that marked Western civilization*** and its first messenger to the Americas, ***Christopher Columbus***."

From the above description of Native Americans before 1776 to being described as ***"merciless Indian Savages"*** in the Declaration of Independence by Thomas Jefferson the author of it in 1776 is deception of the highest order. Native Americans were protecting what was rightfully theirs like we do the USA, a land some have come to believe belongs to Caucasian Americans as it has been implied lately with Barack Obama, who is half-White half-Black, as president, that they want to take back their country because he is really not White.

In the first chapter Howard Zinn, in the "People's History of the United States," further writes about Las Casas, and I quote:

"When he arrived on Hispaniola in 1508, Las Casas says, "there were 60,000 people living on this island, including the Indians; so that from 1494 to 1508, over ***three million people had perished from war, slavery, and the mines***. Who in future generations will believe this? I myself writing it as a knowledgeable eyewitness can hardly believe it. . . ." Thus began the history, five hundred years ago, of the European invasion of the Indian settlements in the Americas. That beginning, when you read Las Casas—even if his figures are exaggerations (were there 3 million Indians to begin with, as he says, or less than a million, as some historians have calculated, or 8 million as others now believe?)—is ***conquest, slavery, death***. When we read the history books given to children in the United States, it all starts with ***heroic adventure—there is no bloodshed***—and ***Columbus Day is a celebration***. Past the elementary and high schools, there are only occasional hints of something else. Samuel Eliot Morison, the

Harvard historian, was the most distinguished writer on Columbus, the author of a multivolume biography, and was himself a sailor who retraced Columbus's route across the Atlantic. In his popular book *Christopher Columbus, Mariner*, written in 1954, he tells about the <u>**enslavement and the killing**</u>: "<u>**The cruel policy initiated by Columbus and pursued by his successors resulted in complete genocide.**</u>" That is on one page, buried halfway into the telling of a grand romance."

For a little while gracious God Almighty allowed America to prosper in spite of its oppression on African Americans, White women, Native Americans, other minorities and Caucasian people considered inferior by the founding fathers. No longer can a righteous and just God Almighty allow this depravity, divisiveness and deception to continue. **THE TIME IS NOW. FOR THE SAKE OF OUR NATION—THE USA.**

Until America frees its citizens from these evils—and I mean all citizens (Black, Brown, Red, Yellow and White), its WOES will continue.

To free these economic and prison captives it will take Almighty God Himself to liberate the slaveholder from the grip of the devil who drives the racist and oppressive slave master.

The U.S. Constitution, as drafted was a snare—a plague or curse to this nation that led to a civil war, which resulted in 625,000 people dead and it was mostly White people.

Abraham Lincoln was forced to free slaves. If it wasn't for the fact that some states had seceded from the union and seized federal property to force a civil war, Lincoln had no intention of abolishing slavery so he can preserve the union as he made it clear in his inaugural address when he became president, Monday, March 4th, 1861, and I quote, **"I have no purpose, directly or indirectly, to interfere with the institution of slavery in the states where it exists. I believe I have no lawful right to do so, and I have no inclination to do so."** Lincoln said he had "**No lawful right to do so**"?

There are Americans who believe their constitutional rights were violated when slavery was abolished, and that sentiment runs deep today in the hearts of some people.

Did Lincoln free the slaves? Technically speaking, no! He was more concerned about the union than the rights of Black people and White women who were property to a few White men. Abraham Lincoln, though, denounced the Dred Scott decision, it would be through the **THIRTEENTH AMENDMENT** that slaves would be freed after over 625,000 people die during the Civil War and President Abraham Lincoln approves the U.S. Constitution 13th amendment.

God Almighty intervened then and He is intervening today 2011 for the 99% and I know so.

Is the Federal government aware, but is ignoring a potentially explosive situation, not to mention God's judgment, which has shown up in the current bubonic plagues we are experiencing today?

As mentioned, a few months ago when I launched my website, I said that, in order for us to remove dysfunction in the US, we are going to need a national revolution and since the ills of exploitative capitalism are affecting the whole planet, we need a global revolution. Today we have "Occupy Wall Street" which has spread through out the United States. The uprisings against corporate greed have been reported in other so-called western "democracies." I saw this coming more so in 2001-2003.

The first **SIXTEEN (16)** presidents condoned slavery. If God hadn't intervened we would still have overt slavery today.

If our leaders, that is, presidents, house reps, senators, governors, mayors, judges, lawyers, law enforcers and every citizen (Black, Brown, Red, Yellow and White) of the United States understood and took to heart what the Bible says and paid attention to events within and outside the U.S. we, the United States, would have prevented the woes at home and abroad we are facing today.

Jeremiah 34:15-18 (NKJV) says and I quote:

"Therefore the word of the Lord came to Jeremiah from the Lord, saying, "Thus says the Lord, the God of Israel: 'I made a covenant with your fathers in the day that I brought them out of the land of Egypt, out of the house of bondage, saying, "At the end of seven years let every man set free his Hebrew brother, who has been sold to him; and when he has served you six years, you shall let him go free from you." But your fathers *did not obey Me nor incline their ear*. Then you recently turned and did what was right in My sight—every man *proclaiming liberty to his neighbor*; and you made a covenant before Me in the house which is called by My name. Then you turned around and *profaned* My name, and every one of you brought back his male and female slaves, whom he had set *at liberty*, at their pleasure, and brought them back *into subjection*, to be your male and female slaves.' "Therefore thus says the Lord: '*You have not obeyed Me in proclaiming liberty, every one* to his *brother* and every one to his *neighbor*. Behold, I proclaim liberty to you,' says the Lord—'to the *sword*, to *pestilence*, and to *famine*! And *I will deliver you to trouble* among *all the kingdoms* of the earth.

And I will give the men who have transgressed My covenant, who have ***not performed*** the words of the covenant which they made before Me, when they cut the calf in two and passed between the parts of it—the ***princes*** of Judah, the princes of Jerusalem, the ***eunuchs***, the ***priests***, and ***all the people*** of the land who passed between the parts of the calf—I will ***give them into the hand of their enemies and into the hand of those who seek their life***. Their dead bodies shall be for meat for the birds of the heaven and the beasts of the earth. And I will give ***Zedekiah king of Judah and his princes*** into the hand of ***their enemies***, into the hand of those ***who seek their life***, and into the hand of the king of Babylon's army which has gone back from you. Behold, I will command,' says the Lord, '***and cause them to return to this city. They will fight against it and take it and burn it with fire***; and I will make the ***cities of Judah a desolation without inhabitant***.'"

Almost everything the above passage is describing has happened in the USA and to the United States—proof that Almighty God is true to His word. Our young men and women are dying in unjust wars being fought because of a dysfunctional foreign policy that has no higher purpose of being blameless and a blessing to all nations on planet earth. "To the ***sword (war)***, to ***pestilence (natural disasters and disease)***, and to ***famine (economic and financial)***! Can we afford a disaster fashioned by the Almighty against us beyond what we are enduring right now? If the answer is no, that is the reason for re-founding the United States.

Madness (Serious Mental Illnesses), Confusion (not knowing what's right), Consumption (HIV/AIDS), Sword (War), famine (Financial Bankruptcy and economic dysfunctions), etc. Predicted In Scripture

In Deuteronomy 28:15-29 (NKJV) it says and I quote:

"But it shall come to pass, if you ***do not obey the voice of the Lord your God***, to observe carefully all His commandments and His statutes which I command you today, that all ***these curses will come upon you and overtake you***: "Cursed *shall* you *be* in the city, and cursed *shall* you *be* in the country. "Cursed *shall be* your basket and your kneading bowl. "Cursed *shall be* the fruit of your body and the produce of your land, the increase of your cattle and the offspring of your flocks. "Cursed *shall* you *be* when you come in, and cursed *shall* you *be* when you go out. "The Lord will send on you ***cursing***, ***confusion***, and ***rebuke*** in all that you set your hand to do, until you are destroyed and until you perish quickly, because of the ***wickedness of your doings in which you have forsaken Me***. The Lord will make the plague cling to you until He has consumed you from the land which you are going to possess. The Lord will strike you with ***consumption***, with fever, with inflammation, with severe burning fever, with the ***sword***, with scorching, and with mildew; they shall pursue you until you perish. ***And your heavens which are over your head shall be bronze, and the earth which is under you shall be iron. The Lord will change the rain of your land to powder*** and dust; from the heaven it shall come down on you until you are destroyed. "The Lord ***will cause you to be defeated before your enemies***; you shall go out one way against them and flee seven ways before them; and you shall become ***troublesome to all the kingdoms of the earth***. Your carcasses shall be food for all the birds of the air and the beasts of the earth, and no one shall frighten *them* away. The Lord will strike you with the boils of Egypt, with tumors, with the scab, and with the itch, from which you cannot be healed. The Lord will strike you with ***madness and blindness and confusion of heart***. And you shall grope at noonday, as a blind man gropes in darkness; ***you shall not prosper in your ways***; you shall be only oppressed and plundered continually, and no one shall save *you.*""

"***Madness and blindness and confusion of heart.......you shall not prosper in your ways.*** That summarizes our situation in the United States and around the world. The word of God is true to the letter, not just as it was to the Hebrews in scripture but to the United States and all nations on the planet today because we are worshippers of the Almighty Dollar and not Almighty God.

When I was falsely accused of mental illness and ended up in mental institutions, I realized God wanted me to see it so I can make this connection of the reality of God's word in our lives today.

And as the fish was to Jonah the prophet so was jail to me. Falsely accused, and ending up in jail, God wanted me to see first-hand how dysfunctional our justice system is and He also wanted to make sure I understood my mission with certainty. Yes like Jonah I was running away from my assignment, but right there in prison God gave me unwavering resolve to ascend to His assignment for me—all for His purpose.

Are we ready to do what is right in the sight of the Almighty? America, we have to be the role model starting NOW!

CHAPTER 11

PRESIDENTIAL CANDIDATES FOR 2012 INCLUDING MR. BARACK OBAMA ARE ILL-EQUIPPED TO FIX WHAT'S WRONG IN THE USA AND AROUND THE PLANET

Again, I am not being an ego-maniac or narcissistic when I say:

Rick Perry—can't match my background.

Mitt Romney—can't match my background.

Michele Bachmann—can't match my background.

Herman Cain—can't match my background.

Newt Gingrich—can't match my background.

Barack Obama—can't match my background.

All other candidates—can't match my background.

You need to know that, this is not about downing others, it is about stating facts based on my education, industry experience, being action and results oriented and above all having visionary leadership and giving all glory to Almighty God, the Creator of the universe. None of the above politicians know what is really wrong. They think it is as easy as cutting taxes and shrinking the size of government—the same old philosophies that haven't worked and will not work—they don't get it. Find out their backgrounds in terms of education and real industry experience—theirs is inadequate in terms of the complexity of issues we have. If all we can create are construction jobs, they are temporary. What next?

I want to lead the United States and the planet to a better place in all essential aspects of life—read my other two books for more insight into our plight today as Americans and citizens of the planet. Do I have all the answers? No. What I have is a framework of systems that can provide opportunity for growth at the individual, corporate, national and global level for all Americans and citizens of the planet of all races, ethnicities, languages, religions, colors and backgrounds.

My background has given me a big picture understanding of how systems interact and what causes dysfunctions and therefore I am better positioned to re-engineer them so they can function as they were intended to by the Designer in the first place. The others don't have my unique problem solving background which I bring to the table of the presidency.

CHAPTER 12

ACT NOW TO AVERT INEVITABLE WORST WORLD WIDE ECONOMIC DISASTERS AND UPRISINGS.

I say, "Real success is deep-rooted in what you can do for others to enhance their lives," and that we must not "wait for tragedy to change our strategy." Now is the time.

The words in the lyrics of TOBYMAC in his song CITY ON OUR KNEES he sings, reiterate *unity*, *love*, *reaching out* and a sense of urgency of *now* as the time for action*, here and across the sea*, saying, and I quote portions of it:

> If you gotta start somewhere
> Why not **here**?
> If you gotta start sometime
> Why not **now**?
> If we gotta start somewhere I say here
> ….
> Through the fog
> There is **hope** in the distance
> From cathedrals to third world missions
> **Love** will fall to the earth like a crashing wave
> Tonight's the night
> For the **sinners** and the **saints**
> Two worlds collide in a beautiful display
> It's all up tonight
> When we **step across the line**
> We can sail **across the sea**
> To a city with one king
> A city on our knees
> Tonight could last forever
> **We are one choice from together**
> **Family, we're family**
> **You and me, yeah you and me**
> If we gotta start somewhere
> Why not **here**?
> If we gotta start sometime

Why not **now**?

No human being past or present has been able to or can change Washington D.C., later on the planet. Even with all my education and industrial experience I can't change Washington D.C. and the planet in my human strength and personal ingeniousness, but I know who we can depend on to accomplish all that needs to be done in the USA and surround the globe. NICOLE C. MULLEN in her song entitled CALL ON JESUS she sings and says, and I quote portions of it:

> I'm so very **ordinary**
> **Nothing special** on my own
> I have **never** walked on water
> I have **never** calmed a storm
> Sometimes I'm hiding away form the madness around me
> Like a child who's afraid of the dark
> But **when I call on Jesus**
> **All things are possible**
> I can mount on wings like eagles and soar
> When I call on Jesus
> Mountains are gonna fall
> **'Cause He'll move heaven and earth to come rescue me when I call**

I hope I have been very clear—my action plan is a framework that is based on free enterprise drawing my reasoning on my:

- extensive education to Ph.D level
- extensive industry and business experience, and
- results and action oriented background

I can guarantee it will work because it is infused with higher purpose—our God-given mission on earth.

Remember it is time for:

SHAEL'S *GLO*(BAL) *RE*(VOLUTION) FOR SHAEL'S *GLORY*

THROUGH THE

F.I.RE—*F.*REEDOM *I.*NDEED *RE.*VOLUTION.

The LORD bless you all and keep you, may the LORD shine His face upon you and be gracious to you, may He lift His countenance upon you and give you peace as we pursue TOTAL FREEDOM for all humanity on the earth:

>Spiritual freedom for all,
>Judicial freedom for all,
>Political freedom for all,
>Educational freedom for all,
>Financial freedom for all,
>Economical freedom for all and
>Social freedom for all.

Tell your friends and family to join us in this global movement—for together we can have it all through the power of the Almighty.

"Real success is deep rooted in what you can do for others to enhance their lives." RJJKM
"Don't wait for tragedy to change your strategy." RJJKM

For more information and to purchase resources, products and services to help you help yourself and others in all essential areas of life go to my website at:

http://www.RonexOnline.Com.

Your beloved friend
Ronex James John Kennedy Muteshael, Ph.D. (Engg-abd)
B.Min.Sc. (Eng), M.Sc.(Engg), M.Sc.(O.M.-abt), Ph.D. (Engg-abd)

For speaking engagements call: 708-582-2584
Or
e-mail request to: ronexkm@gmail.com

www.ingramcontent.com/pod-product-compliance
Lightning Source LLC
Chambersburg PA
CBHW080948170526
45158CB00008B/2414